Conditions for
Becoming a Democratic State

Conditions for Becoming a Democratic State

Edited by

Samar Kumar Mondal

Suryodaya Books

Cataloging in Publication Data — DK
[Courtesy: D.K. Agencies (P) Ltd. <docinfo@dkagencies.com>]

Conditions for becoming a democratic state /
edited by Samar Kumar Mondal.
pages cm
"... outcome of the departmental seminar proceedings under the CAS programme of the University Grants Commission" – Preface.
Includes bibliographical references.
ISBN 9788193607657

1. Democracy – India – History – Congresses. I. Mondal, Samar Kumar, 1974- editor. II. Jadavpur University. Department of Philosophy, publisher.

LCC JQ281.C66 2021 | DDC 320.954 23

ISBN: 978-81-936076-5-7
First published in India in 2023

Published by:
Department of Philosophy
Jadavpur University
Kolkata - 700032

and

Suryodaya Books
Suryodaya, D-36A/1, Mohan Garden
Najafgarh Road, New Delhi - 110059
Phone : 9871394811

Distributed by:
D.K. Printworld (P) Ltd.
Regd. Office : "Vedaśrī", F-395, Sudarshan Park
ESI Hospital Metro Station, New Delhi - 110015
Phones : (011) 2545 3975, 2546 6019
e-mail : indology@dkprintworld.com
Web : www.dkprintworld.com

Printed by: Suryodaya Books, New Delhi

Preface

THIS volume is an outcome of the departmental seminar proceedings under the Centre for Advanced Study (CAS) programme of the University Grants Commission (UGC). Our thanks are due to the UGC for funding this project.

Some of the articles of this volume are a product of group discussion held regularly during the last five years. We have tried to arrive at a particular conclusion regarding the conditions for becoming a democratic state. The members of this group have chosen different areas of democracy for the purpose of exploring the field. I would like to thank all the members of the heterogeneous group for extending their help, academic as well as non-academic, towards the publication of this book. I would like to take this opportunity to thank all our colleagues whose concern and inspiration of thought-provoking comments from time to time have made the publication of this book possible.

I would also like to acknowledge my gratitude towards Professor Soumitra Basu of the Department of Philosophy, Jadavpur University and Professor Sadhan Chakraborti, Hon'ble Vice-Chancellor of Kazi Nazrul University, Asansol, for their valuable suggestions.

I am also grateful to Shri Rajendra Agarwal of Suryodaya Books for publication of this volume in an attractive way.

Jadavpur
March 2021

Samar Kumar Mondal

Contents

Preface v

Introduction 1

1. Decoding Democracy 11
   – *Jyotish Chandra Basak*

2. On Infringement upon Democratic Rights 37
   – *Kausik Bhattacharya*

3. Kauṭilya and His Arthaśāstra: A Notion of Democracy in Ancient Indian Society 43
   – *Projit Kumar Palit*

4. Problem of Democracy and Its Effects on Human Rights 63
   – *Samar Kumar Mondal*

5. Norms of Democracy in Buddhist Thought: Ideas and Implementation 75
   – *Gouri Sankar Bandyopadhyay*

6. Quest for the Responsibilities to Make an Ideal Democratic State 95
   – *Rajkumar Modak*

7. Created Leadership, Power and Ethics: A Critical Analysis 115
   – *Tapan Kumer De*

Contributors 137

Index 139

will always be peace in that state. As a result, the governance of the state will be permanent. People should keep an eye on the rulers to ensure that they govern the state efficiently. It is said that "governance of the state" can be an important discussion of state and also an important area of social philosophy.

The question may arise: is there any standard on the basis of which good governance of a state can be established? We find different interpretations of good governance in the East and the West. For example, in the East, as a system of good governance, monarchy was considered good form of governance. In the same way, the West too considered monarchy as a good means of governance. Again, someone has tried to explain good governance through three regimes (monarchy, aristocracy and rule of law), such as Aristotle's idea of state. Over the past decade, democracy and democratic values have come to the brink of extinction around the world, especially in the third-world countries. In particular, in the context of democracy in our country, it has become more complex, which has left a scar on the foreheads of democracy-loving and peace-loving people. Because, its value and the rule of the people are often overlooked. However, the democratic system is the most popular among the various systems of government in the modern world and most of the countries in the world have adopted this system. It is also true that democracy is not completely flawless. However, its benefits outweigh the disadvantages. People's lack of proper knowledge about democracy, lack of democratic mindset and self-centredness have thrown third-world countries like India into a serious social and political crisis.

Plato mentions in his *Republic*:

> Administration is an art that cannot be understood by ordinary people. Only intelligent and capable people can realize this.

In fact, there is no substitute for education to make a person extraordinary, intelligent and capable. Only when the people of the society or state are enlightened as a result of education, knowledge will, all the positive efforts, including democracy, be successful. Basically, backwardness in the field of education, lack of awareness, crisis of values and, above all, the triumph of degradation has put democracy in a serious crisis. Just as it is not reasonable to blame a particular group for this, we, as a nation, are responsible for this jeopardy.

All of us have an intuitive idea about democracy. The term "democracy" first appeared in ancient Greek political and philosophical thought of the city-state of Athens during classical antiquity. Cleisthenes, an ancient lawgiver, is referred to as "the father of Athenian democracy". Though this concept was a subject matter of the Greek society, it was also seen in the Indian scenario. No consensus exists on how to define democracy, but legal equality, freedom and rule of law have been identified as its important characteristics since ancient times. These principles are reflected in all eligible citizens being equal before the law and having equal access to legislative processes. For example, in a representative democracy, every vote has equal weight, no unreasonable restrictions can apply to anyone seeking to become a representative, and the freedom of its eligible citizens is secured by legitimized rights and liberties which are typically protected by a constitution.

One theory holds that democracy requires three fundamental principles:

1. upward control, i.e. sovereignty residing at the lowest levels of authority,
2. political equality, and
3. social norms by which individuals and institutions consider acceptable acts that reflect the first two principles of upward control and political equality.

Democracy contrasts with other forms of government where power is either held by one person, as in monarchy, or where power is held by a small number of individuals, as in oligarchy.

Nevertheless, these oppositions, inherited from Greek philosophy, are now ambiguous because contemporary governments have mixed democratic, oligarchic and monarchic elements. Karl Popper defined democracy in contrast to dictatorship or tyranny, thus focusing on opportunities for the people to control their leaders and to oust them without the need for a revolution.

Several variants of democracy exist, but there are two basic forms, one is direct and the other is representative democracy, and both concern how the whole body of all eligible citizens executes its will.

Democracy is a form of government in which all eligible citizens participate equally either directly or indirectly through elected representatives in the proposal, development and creation of laws. It encompasses social, economic and cultural conditions that enable the free and equal practice of political self-determination.

We want to live in a state or society where every person should get equal treatment and equal rights. No man wants to live in an autocratic state or society. Today we are facing many problems in a democratic state. That is why this question arises: is there anything wrong with the idea of democracy? The existence of political parties is essential for democracy. Consequently, on an occasion democracy has been threatened by the political parties themselves. As we live in a representative democratic state, we sent our representatives who are expected to act for the welfare of the society. But, most of the time, they encourage their followers to conduct strikes, bandhs, road jams, etc. In most of the cases, people do not support these activities, as they have to face many bad consequences of these activities. It may be that no political leader or representative does support these activities from her/his own heart. But they cannot express their disagreement as the person comes under the parasol of a political party and the party calls for such negative impacting activity.

Again, one of the important characteristics of democracy is

the rule of majority. A decision on a particular issue is decided on the basis of the opinion of the majority of people and the opinion of the minority is ignored. This gives rise to the autocratic rule of the majority.

It is now time to discuss about the concept of democracy and its implementation in our country. Regarding the problems of democracy, a number of questions arise. Is it the problem of implementation? Or is it the problem of method by which democracy is implemented? Or is it the problem of the concept of democracy?

The essay entitled "Decoding Democracy" tries to trace the basic fabrics of democracy. We come across various shades of democracy in different parts of the globe and also that existed at different times of known history. The author recounts them briefly and makes efforts to give a minimalist interpretation of the concept of democracy. Following Sir Karl Popper, he reformulates the basic question of democracy and tries to show that the commonly held view that a democratic system empowers people is prima facie a leading view, but it is not the right one. However, the popularity of this form of governance is derived not from its own merits but from the depravity of other known and practised forms of governance. He also shows that how the parliamentary form of democracy, which has been called the "end of history" by Francis Fukuyama, is a flawed one and brings to our notice Jacques Derrida's critique of it. How identity politics caused havoc on some ideologies and sent them to the backburner has also been discussed by the author. He ends his article with a positive note that only through trial and error we can usher in a better system and mistakes are an indispensable part of any system-improvement mechanism.

The paper entitled "On Infringement upon Democratic Rights" deals with showing how infringement takes place on democratic rights. Most of the time we have seen that human rights are violated in different ways. The question is: what are the reasons

Introduction

> Man is by nature a social animal; an individual who is unsocial naturally and not accidentally is either beneath our notice or more than human. Society is something that precedes the individual. Anyone who either cannot lead the common life or is so self-sufficient as not to need to, and therefore does not partake of society, is either a beast or a god. – Aristotle, *Politics*

HUMAN beings are naturally social animals and that is why they cannot live outside of the umbrella of the so-called society. Generally a society is made up of some families and a state gets formed when some societies come together with their positive effort. So, there is a deep connection among the people, societies and a state. People are interdependent, so they cannot live without the other. Therefore, a state cannot be formed without societies and the formation of a state remains incomplete without a social structure.

Now the question naturally arises: what is the necessity to form a state? Just as people always want to lead a good life and man cannot fulfil her/his natural requirements without the help of others, the need for a state emerges. Similarly, a person moves forward with an ideology in order to lead a proper life in the society. That is why a state moves forward with an ideology in mind for the welfare of the people. Consequently, the main task of a state is to ensure that its people live peacefully and no person commits any wrongdoing. Because, if a person commits any crime or wrongdoing that harms another person in the society. The offender will be given exemplary punishment for that act, so that no other person in the society does that kind of crime. The state will punish the wrongdoer for maintaining peace, tranquility and the growth of the society. In other words, the state will monitor and curb the crimes of its people in order to lead the society in the right direction. Therefore, it can be said that the state is the driving force of the society.

In a situation where a state does not govern its society properly, its citizens cannot live a healthy life and they will fail to accomplish their normal needs. Only the state can meet the natural needs of the individuals through efficient governance. Not only that, if there is no governance, there will be no laws and discipline in the society. And one will not hesitate to do any kind of harm to another if there is no proper governance in the state. This kind of activity may continue due to the lack of proper laws or governance in the society or state. If people want to maintain the prosperity and growth of a society, they have to obey and maintain the rules laid out by the state; otherwise, there will be no equality in that state, consequently. It will be a state consisting of irrational or inhuman beings. So, it is very important to have governance in the state and the state has to enhance humanity and also rationality among its people through proper policies and laws.

This regime can be of two types. Good governance and/or bad governance. A system of governance, run by a ruler or a few individuals, that results in the misery of the common man can be called a bad regime. If there is such a system of governance in a state, that state cannot last long. In such a situation, the common man tries to leave this kind of governance and stay under good governance. Good governance is a system of governance that conducts its affairs for the benefit of the people without thinking of its own interests, resulting in the wholesome welfare of the people. If a state has this kind of governance in place, every person in it will be able to fulfil her/his dreams. Guided with honesty and devotion, its citizens will be able to perform their duties independently. When the people of a state live well, air their views freely and enjoy their freedom for the overall benefit of the total populace, then there behind the violation of human rights? Philosophers are the right or authentic persons to enquire into this problem and find answers to it, because thought experience is much needed in answering this question. An ideal democratic state is that where the violation of democratic rights seldom occurs. But when any political party violates people's democratic rights, judiciary is the only way to protect such rights, but when judiciary becomes corrupt then people try to reformulate their rights through media and when media leaves their impartial nature, people do not have any way to reformulate or protect their rights. Any advanced democracy wants to have growth, prosperity, etc. instead of corruption or political terrorism and the main characteristics of any advanced democracy is the existence of a smaller number of committed voters. In any advanced democracy, there must be more than one political party and one of them is selected by the people casting their vote. This is the actual scenario of any democratic state. But the question is: whom can I cast my vote if all political representatives are corrupt? In that case, the honourable Supreme Court of India has allowed the voters to exercise "no choice" or "none of the above option", but if "no choice" option has obtained the number of majority votes, then what will be the next step? In that case, the honourable Supreme Court has not specified, as what has to be done in such a situation.

The paper "Kauṭilya and His Arthaśāstra: A Notion of Democracy in Ancient Indian Society" emphasizes on the root of democracy in Indian political thought. Although some people believe that the concept of democracy was developed by the Western thinkers, such as Plato and Aristotle, it was a serious subject matter of Indians even before the Greeks and there is no doubt about it. Although Kauṭilya's concept of state is fundamentally monarchical, he developed a welfare state consisting of legal equality, freedom and rule of law. While studying his work, at we will see that there were roots of democratic system in any given society. He actually started the political thought of Realism. Kauṭilya's Arthaśāstra is the art of diplomacy and thus he opines that the happiness of a king depends on the happiness of his subjects.

The paper entitled "Problem of Democracy and Its Effects on Human Rights" explores the problem of democracy from different philosophical perspectives. Democracy and human rights are close and complementary to each other. Basically, the main goal of democracy is to ensure human rights. Therefore, it is impossible to establish real democracy without practising human rights. From the very beginning of civilization, every human being has been thinking of his/her rights and development. Gradually people have become more aware of their rights through intellectual practice and also from moral perspectives. That is why people have always been vocal in demanding the establishment of human rights. Whenever there was disrespect for human rights in the world, various kinds of revolutions and wars took place. Human rights and democracy are the essence of a modern welfare state. As a citizen of the state, every human being wants his basic rights and thereby social security. People want impartial justice and indeed the rule of law. In this paper, thc author has tried to explain the relation between democracy and human rights and the different problems of it and finally tries to reach a plausible solution to it.

"Norms of Democracy in Buddhist Thought: Ideas and Implementation" expounds on the noble ideas of the basic forms of democracy from the Buddhist point of view. Buddhism is the oldest of the world religions and has played a major role in the history and culture of entire Asia, similar to that of Islam in the Middle East and North Africa. Buddhism emerged around three jewels (*triratna*) — Buddha, Dharma (canonical rules) and the Saṅgha (congregation). The present study humbly attempts to review the basic democratic as well as socialistic ideas of Gautama Buddha, the founder of Buddhism which got reflected in his Saṅgha, the classless, casteless democratic, monastic organization. The focal theme of the Buddhist religion was "welfare and happiness of the majority of population" (*bahujanahitāya, bahujanasukhāya ...*). Saṅgha had become largely a semi-autonomous, self-regulatory and socio-religious–monastic organization. Lord Buddha asked the people to join the Saṅghas which was mostly modelled on the pattern of previous decadent tribal democracies emerged in early northern India. He was full of reverence for the ancestral institutions — the *gaṇas* or Saṅghas (older republics), existed in the sixth century BCE in India and which became the prototype of his own monastic order. There were a lot of rules and regulations regarding the voting procedure and the quorum of the Buddhist Order. The Buddha himself had deep concern for inner-Saṅgha democracy. As he did not nominate any successor, the monks living within a defined boundary elected their respective chiefs (*saṅghatthera* or *saṅghaparināyaka*) democratically. The paper further argues that the Buddha had become the messiah of a bulk of poor, downtrodden and marginal population of his times rejecting socio-economic inequality and exploitation. One of the Buddhist innovations was the opening of membership of the Order (Saṅgha) to all genders, castes and classes. Again, he felt firmly against private property and individual possession within the Order. Early Buddhist scriptures like the *Dīgha Nikāya* record the Buddha's attitude towards imperialistic aggression and expansion. Major factors behind the success of early Buddhism were the monastic code of disciplines (Vinaya ritual and traditions) and its inherent egalitarian and democratic ideology. The Buddha worked to build up a model society placing his Saṅgha in centre which would be free from all vices such as caste–class consciousness, greed, exploitation and anti-democratic authoritarian practices.

The article "Quest for the Responsibilities to Make an Ideal Democratic State" explains the responsibilities of a ruler or political parties in any democratic system. Responsibilities can be explained from different perspectives like authority, a fare election, freedom, equality, human rights, proper activity and application of law, values of tolerance and education. Education is the most important factor for establishing actual democracy in any civil society. That is why Plato said that philosophers should take the charge of rules that is called "Philosopher King". Because, only philosophers can show the right way to the growth of a society or a state.

"Created Leadership, Power and Ethics: A Critical Analysis" explores the ethical norms of a leader and the activities according to the norms, or not. A leader must have to follow the norms set by the concept of ethics at the time of exercising power. In democratic field, the ethics of responsibility must be followed. If any leader fails to do his/her job following the concept of ethics of responsibility, he/she is considered as a leader without goal. Traditional leadership, charismatic leadership and legal-rational leadership as defined by Max Weber are successful leaderships in democracy as these all intend to follow the norms of the ethics of responsibility. At present, a new trend of leadership emerged in the last part of the last century in India. The trend is to handover the power to the future generations without listening to the voice of his/her followers. This new kind of leadership is called created leadership. The question is that is it possible for a created leader to exercise political power in accordance with the concept of ethics of responsibility?

1

Decoding Democracy

Jyotish Chandra Basak

How the entity called state has come into being is an intriguing question. In ancient India we find one sort of explanation; in modern times Western thinkers gave a distinct hypothesis. In whatever way or for whatever reasons it has emerged, the next prime concern for philosophers was about its administration. It is in this context that the notion of good government and bad government has drawn the attention of thoughtful minds. Among the known form of political regimes, it is widely believed that democracy is the most popular one. One of the reasons for its acceptance and admiration is the ideology on which this political order is based upon.

Of the many tasks performed by the political philosophy, the foremost is to describe and evaluate political ideologies. One reason for our concern with political ideologies is that it affects everybody's life significantly as we live under one form of government or the other, following one particular ideology. The Italian painter Ambrogio Lorenzetti in his celebrated mural, drawn sometime between 1337-39, entitled the "Allegory of Good and Bad Government", depicted beautifully the qualities that good rulers should have and bad qualities that they should not have. Hence, it is no wonder that political philosophers from ancient time till today kept themselves engaged with the discussion of ideologies and made efforts to lay down conditions of good government.

Among the political ideologies or orders so far invented and practised, democracy is the most commended one in contemporary politics. Though it has been opined by some thinkers (e.g. Bertrand Russell) that it is the anarchism (advocated by Mikhail Aleksandrovich Bakunin, a nineteenth-century political writer, and Peter Kropotkin, a twentieth-century activist and writer who articulated this political order with great care) that is the ideal form of political order but many thinkers expressed their misgivings about the practice of this form in current time or in foreseeable future. Democracy as a political order has attracted much attention in current discussion for some reason or other. It is widely acknowledged that it is the best form of government and any deviation from the democratic procedure is greeted with a loud cry from a cross-section of people. Francis Fukuyama held that it is almost impossible to improve upon the current form of electoral parliamentary democracy. His terming it the "end of history" and the "end of ideological conflict" evoked a sharp response from critics and one such critic was Jacques Derrida about whom we intend to discuss later on. It is indeed a fact that in our age when a country claims to be a democratic one, by and large, it boasts of its form in contemporary political deliberations.

However, when we try to understand what is meant by democracy, we get baffled. There are so many variations in its practice throughout the globe and at different times that we start thinking about its real characteristics. On account of its numerous forms, it becomes difficult to offer a minimalist interpretation of this political order that can be considered as its essence. Therefore, it appears to our mind that the explanation of democracy or discussion of its essential traits also demands a democratic frame of mind — acceding a variety of forms within its compass. Let us get a bird's-eye view of some of its forms.

A survey of its form gives us a list of at least six types of democratic structures. Direct democracy is one such type. In such governance, all adult people participate in deliberations and decision making. Such ilk of democracy was practised in ancient Greece and sporadically at some other places, e.g. in some Swiss cantons. Joseph Alois Schumpeter, a political economist of Harvard University, who is known for popularizing the concept of "creative destruction" advocated a form of democracy in his book *Capitalism, Socialism and Democracy* (1943). His notion of democracy in the aforesaid book is thus:

> It is the institutional arrangement for arriving at political decisions in which individuals acquire the power to decide by means of a competitive struggle for people's vote. – 1943: 269

A study of his definition makes it clear that he has done away with characteristics such as accountability, liberty, equality, representation and other similar characteristics which people think are embedded in this type of statecraft. In many respects, he agreed with Marx that capitalism will ultimately crumble and will be supervened upon by socialism. But he disagreed with Marx about the process of collapse, as for him, it will not be overthrown by violent revolution, rather capitalism will slowly erode and in due course will be replaced by socialism. Another form of democracy is known as populist democracy. In such type of democracy people (or their popular leader) rule themselves rather than by a selected minority or by some external force. In such a system, the ruler must act as per popular will. Liberal democracy is another dominant form. In this type of democracy, some basic values are given overriding importance instead of the popular will. John Rawls, in his *A Theory of Justice* (1971), identifies some such supreme values. Supporters of this type are more concerned to ensure the preclusion of public officials from taking advantage of power for wrong reasons. Participatory democracy is another model which was advocated for getting rid of drawbacks of other types. Supporters of this kind of democracy observe that many modern democracies are facing a bizarre problem. They consider the political apathy of common citizens to political issues is caused by numerous factors. They attribute these factors to the non-participation of the common man in political matters. Hence, they hold that active participation of masses in political decision making will enhance their interest on crucial issues and also boost their curiosities. Akin to liberal democracy is social democracy though it has its own identity. It is more comprehensive in the sense that some domains which liberals considered private and hence not to be interfered with, social democrats try to enter into those so-called private domains. For example, economic exercises and families are some domains where they think democratization is required. And finally, deliberative democracy is a kind which accords importance to popular will but for this, they hold deliberations indispensable. And deliberations entail personal autonomy. In brief, it is a blend of liberal and populist democracy.

Another mystery is the origin of the political dispensation under discussion. It is widely agreed that it saw its early manifestation in ancient Greece. Though we find references that Sumer, in the ancient Mesopotamian province, had developed governance like primitive democracy, it could not attract much attention. Victor Ehrenberg holds that

> [the] Greeks were the first political people in the history of mankind, for they were the first to create states purely as communities of citizens in which the administration and the making of policy were the right and the duty of these citizens.
>
> – 1950: 515

In this statement, the crux is "administration and the making of policy were the right and duty of these citizens". This may be taken as the core characteristic of democracy. The earliest documentary proof we get about the evolution of democratic administration is *The Suppliants*, the most ancient extant Greek play written in the fifth century BCE by Aeschylus. There we find that in one of the oldest cities of Greece, Argos, King Pelasgus developed, in all practical purposes, a form of rule which may be termed democratic. In matters of importance, which affected the whole community, the king discussed them with his citizens. Though he was the ruler, he did not act without consulting dēmos, i.e. common people. Pelasgus appears to hold that he is not an independent ruler as his position is derived from a specific constitution of the state. He considered himself as leader of his citizens who are ready to follow his guidance but he is decrepit without his citizens' endorsement or authorization and this endorsement he did not consider as already given on all issues. He further considered the democratic form of government as a requirement for making a decision — a decision which is a responsible one and not a whimsical verdict. But it is Athens that stole the limelight and hence it is widely held that democratic set-up of government had its seat there first. Leo Strauss's writing also substantiates our claim. In any way, setting aside the controversy about a specific region of its origin we can say that it was in ancient Greece that this type of statecraft first unfolded.

The notion of democracy that we are talking of is about political organization, statecraft or mode of governance. It can be contrasted with other forms of governance such as oligarchy, aristocracy, monarchy and many other forms of governance. But over time, the term (i.e. democracy) assumed some dimensions which have bearing on social justice. Thinkers are prone to call them democratic ideals or principles. Some of the ideals which are inextricably related to it are liberty, equality, justice, fraternity, tolerance, reason and variety. When we find any of these elements lacking in society, we are prone to call it undemocratic. Thus, it becomes evident that some social ideals having ethical overtones have become an essential part of the term "democracy". On account of the appealing nature of these ideals and form of governance, even the term democracy is appended before other forms of political practice such as socialism, e.g. democratic socialism. Even some communist countries find it enticing to call their form of governance people's democracy. Over time, it has assumed so many dimensions that expressions "democratic culture", "democratic attitude", etc. have become fashionable in common parlance.

An inevitable question that arises in our mind is why as social ideal the term "democratic" has gained so much acceptance. For Macpherson, for times it gives the impression that this governmental set-up contains everything "that is humanly good". To my mind, democratic set-up of government ensures opportunities that are very close to the aspirations of modern man. These aspirations are certain liberal attitudes that they harbour so fondly. As these ideals are mostly the characteristics of liberalism, democratic states are also sometimes termed "liberal states". Some ideas that are found in liberalism and also common in a democracy are freedom, equality, justice, toleration, individual and group identity, and recognition of certain rights. These ideals are indeed captivating but they are intricate and also contested. These ideals of liberalism cannot be practised in many other forms of state organizations. They

> require a certain form of state, that is, one in which institutions have specified roles and functions, such as making laws or implementing justice, with specified relationships between the main institutions of state so that none of them can dominate the others. – Sivaramakrishnan 2017: 31

Historically liberalists first focused on constitutional government and then gradually on representative government as such. In such a governmental form, its power is moderated by laws and hence precludes arbitrary or tyrannical rule. Impartial judiciary further ensures that checks and balances are in place. Though it is right that values of liberalism have a close rapport with modern democracy or representative government, yet we should not forget that there are several unsettled tensions between these two. Liberal theorists are always anxious with a hunch in their mind that institutions created under this form of governance can go beyond their intended boundary and thus can inappropriately take advantage of their power. Despite this fear and other tensions between liberalism and democracy affinity between these two is writ large.

Let us get a glimpse of the might of the ideals of democracy. The Burmese leader Aung San Suu Kyi struggled for democracy in her country and she delineated her striving in her famous book *Freedom from Fear*. Again, the South African leader Nelson Mandela who also fought for liberty, equality and justice scribed his long struggle in his *Long Walk to Freedom* (1994). These and many such fascinating writings make us think that we put a premium on values like freedom, liberty and equality. We consider these as inalienable to our being. It brings us scope, as Suu Kyi says, to lead a dignified human life. Moreover, as an ideal "freedom", when contrasted with setting free from all restrictions and discriminations, in all sphere of life (though was repugnant to Plato), is so attractive that though we know of its unattainability still, as Subhas Chandra Bose held, satisfies the craving of the soul. Again, equality is an ideal thirst for which a simple man sacrificed his tranquil life and ultimately transformed himself to "Mahatma". Inequality or unfairness is a ubiquitous phenomenon. It is manifested in innumerable dimensions – property, treatment, privileges and so on. Struggling lives of Mahatma Gandhi and Martin Luther King Jr exemplify how dearly people value the ideal of equality. Both these – equality and liberty – ideals are inseparably related to the notion of justice. Any effort to restrict these ideals is considered undemocratic. Another ideal, entangled with democracy, is fraternity. For D.D. Raphael it (fraternity) "expresses the idea of common responsibility, responsibility for others. ..." (2009: 86). Thus, we find that all these ideals – liberty, equality, toleration and fraternity – attracted enlightened human mind. Hence, it is not surprising that the term "democracy" or qualification "democratic" will be liked by most of people. Democracy as a political order promotes these ideals or at least thought to be creating an ambience where people can approximate towards these ideals. For example, in a democratic system nowadays every adult citizen is granted the voting right and each vote has equal value irrespective of other qualifications. Hence, it is held that it a basic step towards achieving equality.

When we consider democracy as political order we find so many variations in its different manifestations, and of which we had a brief look in a previous passage, we wonder about its essential features. In other words, when can we say that a system is a democracy and another one is not? In order to say this, we need to identify some of its essential characters. However, explanations of its essential characters got changed with time as thinkers found that interpretations are not encompassing enough to capture its essence. Let us see whether an etymological study of the term "democracy" can help us excavate its essential characters. We come to know that the term at last analysis originated from the Greek term *dēmokratia* which is a combination of *dēmos* meaning the people and *kratia* meaning power, rule, etc. From this etymological explanation we can make a naive view that in such a political organization people rule themselves, i.e. they hold the power. The 16th President of the United States of America Abraham Lincoln, a wise statesman who led the country at a very critical time, in his Gettysburg Address delivered on 19 November 1863, and also even two years before this (1861), said something of this political arrangement which have become so oft-quoted that every man who takes interest about this form of governance know this. In that speech, he couched the quintessential components of this political order very succinctly. Taking from his speech we can say that it is a form of self-government. It is a form of governance, as he said in 1861, "a government of the people, by the same people". It underlines the idea that all men are created equal. In the conclusion of the Gettysburg Address he held that it is the government "of the people, by the people, and for the people ...". Thus, we can say that in a democracy people hold the steering and decide its direction. It enhances their choice and in turn liberty. It, of course, entails responsible actions from its citizens. Thus, this classic address tells us that people's participation in decision-making process shapes the core of democracy.

If it is the people who exercise power in a democracy, the

debatable point then is how do people participate in governance and how effective is their participation. Here becomes the relevance of the distinction between direct democracy and representative democracy. In a direct democracy, people's participation took place directly, as we have seen previously, in some ancient small states. But even this participation was not of all citizens. For example, we come to know that in ancient Athens, when it practised direct democracy, women and slaves were not allowed to participate in deliberations. Another form of democracy widely practised in the modern era is representative democracy. In such a system people choose its representative to act on his/her behalf. But the evolution of a strong party system has taken away scope for a representative to express either the view of people or his/her own. Edmund Burke, a noted political thinker of the eighteenth century, made the famous distinction between "representative" and "delegate". For him, in democracy, a delegate only reproduces or echoes the views given by people of his/her constituency whereas a representative instead of reproducing this applies his judgement. The term "judgement" is an intricate one as it involves within it a number of issues. In coming to a political judgement, the representative needs to take into account factual information, moral grounds and people's conflicting views/choices. All of these elements are important. The representative has to judge fallout of choosing an alternative rather than another one. This is part of the factual component. As a representative represents diverse social classes, he/she needs to judge the strength of the views of his/her people. Majority/minority dichotomy is a crucial factor as it might give rise to quantity/quality chasm. The choice of the crowd may not always be qualitatively superior to the minority's view. Hence, the representative has to judge whether the minority's view should override the qualitatively low majority's view. Moral consideration is another important component in making a political judgement. It might be argued that all politicians, i.e. representatives, may not have sound knowledge of appropriate moral principles involved with an issue under consideration. Still, it is held that "there is likely to be a large measure of agreement on the basic principle of life in a democratic society" (Miller 2003: 46). The convolution of these elements in political judgement places a lot of responsibility on representatives.

The system of governance through representatives, though indeed appealing, is facing hosts of questions as the "people" and their "power" which are at the core are facing a robust challenge in the modern-day's brawny party system. Since representatives are elected on some or other party's pass, they have little scope either to act on the basis of views expressed by their electors or exercise their own political judgement. A representative merely acts as a minion of his/her party's boss. The representative hardly listens to his/her voters or acts on his/her conscience. He/she rather tries to propagandize his/her party line of thinking and tries to indoctrinate his/her electors accordingly. Hence, people and their power become inconsequential and become relevant only after the stipulated period when the next voting takes place. Even there is no guarantee that majority electors' opinion will be a deciding factor during an election, e.g. in more-than-the-two-party system the winner may not garner majority's support. Thus, doubt is expressed whether people are at the core as the etymology of the term "democracy" suggests. Burke's distinction of a delegate and a representative has thus become somewhat blunt.

On account of the aforesaid problem with the interpretation, we find Sir Karl Popper is not ready to regard democracy as the rule of the people. Drawing from the history of its origin Popper holds that the question at the centre of the discussion on governance is an issue which began with Plato's writings. The paramount question was: who should rule (a state)? In Plato's time, the inquiry was: is it the best (as happens in monarchy), or the best few (in aristocracy) or by many (as happens in a democracy)? Plato favoured the best of all or the best of few, but not many (i.e. *dēmos*). Marx gave a twist to the issue by advocating that it is to be done by the working class. Before Plato, Athenians practised direct democracy. But he was not happy with the state of affairs there and could foresee the pitfalls of this system and hence he did not favour this system of governance. As it happened, Plato was born during the Peloponnesian War which continued for almost twenty-eight years, with some interruptions, between Sparta and Athens. He was about twenty-four years old when it ended. He saw its terrible effects on the people of Athens which made him disgusted about this sort of political arrangement.

Thus, the principle of legitimacy of ruling that attracted the attention of contemplative minds kept evolving over ages due to various dynamics. Popper in his *The Open Society and Its Enemies* (1988) put forward what he considers a more realistic alternative to the above-stated issue. In criticizing Plato's view about political establishment, he showed what caused Plato to denounce democracy. Popper firmly disagreed with Plato and resolutely believed that despite its many drawbacks, democracy only can ensure an open society. In such a system, the critics of democracy are not its enemies. This differentiates democracy from a totalitarian state. In 1988, in his article in *The Economist* Popper reformulated the central question about this political regime as: how can a state be formed so that an unacceptable ruler can be removed without bloodbath or force? This is the central question of this political order and democratic form provides an answer to this as it is possible to remove the ruler by the majority's vote. In spite of a more plausible solution given by his reformulated question, Popper holds that democracy tempts us to ideologies that are unattainable as in no modern democracy people are by rights "the real and ultimate and the only legitimate rulers". In practice, it is only a few people in government or its ancillaries that rule. Still, Popper believes that although democracy may not be a rule of the demos still there is found a pronounced rule of the law that posits ways for the removal of an unwelcome government without a bloodbath. Though it is through the majority's votes that an unwanted government is got rid of, Popper does not hold that majority's decision is always or usually be a right one. In spite of having all these imperfections, he, almost like Winston Churchill, opine that though it is a deficient form of governance still it is worth fighting for and dying for as it provides a way for the dismissal of a government without resorting to violent means. It can best be understood by someone who resided under a different political order. To put it in a different way, it is not the goodness of the system, rather, the wickedness of other systems till now we learnt that provides the substratum for favouring democracy.

"Is the form of governance through representatives (in a democracy) legitimate?" was another question that Popper (1988) addressed. Speaking in favour of proportional representation he holds that such representation gives out to political parties some sort of constitutional standing. But he vacillates about the rightness and viability of such representation. In such a system, he writes:

> ... I can choose only a party. And the people who may represent the party are chosen only by the party. And while people and their opinions always deserve the greatest respect, the opinions adopted by parties (which are typically instruments of personal advancement and of power, with all the chances for intrigue which this implies) are not to be identified with ordinary human opinions: they are ideologies.

Where there is no party system, the representative is personally accountable to his people. Again, opining against such strong party systems which enslave representatives he writes:

> ... the system under which he was elected robs him of personal responsibility; it makes him a voting machine rather than a thinking and feeling person. ... For what we need in politics are individuals who can judge on their own and who are prepared to carry personal responsibility.

In spite of this strongly-worded criticism of proportional representation, Popper realized that it is indeed difficult to find a representative who is ready to exercise his/her judgement and also it is a fact that we could not conceive of a party-less democracy.

Hence, he favours the "trial and error" method and hoped that with effecting corrections of existing blemishes we shall be able to improve upon current democratic dispensation. He considered any radical change for bringing about a perfect arrangement of governance is fraught with dangers. Mistakes are inevitable parts of our experiments with social engineering. Hence, like Plato, he did not favour the political programme of creating a perfect society.

In representative forms of governance, we find different types of party system. In some countries, there exists the two-party system, whereas in some other more-than-two-party system. Both these systems have positive as well as negative sides. For Popper, the positive side of many parties is that it offers "more choice, more opportunities, less rigidity, more criticism". It, in turn, entails "greater distribution of influence and power". In spite of these advantages, it has many downsides. For example, it happens more often than not that a number of parties enter into a deal for the formation of a government and such coalition comes into existence with its host of difficulties. In several cases, a small party can exert disproportionate influence. Again, there is corrosion of responsibility for members of the coalition partners. Next, voting out of office is another problem as there are many parties; voters remain in suspense which party will be in office in next term. As Popper (1988) says:

> ... on election day none of the parties is dismissed, none is convicted. Accordingly, nobody looks on election day as a Day of Judgement, as a day when the responsible government stands to account for its deeds and omissions, for its successes and failures, and a responsible opposition criticizes this record and explains what steps the government ought to have taken, and why.

About the advantage of the two-party system, Popper holds that it provides the scope of self-criticism as the defeated party considers it imperative for dissecting where things have gone wrong and this self-reflection makes room for effecting the necessary corrections. Again, it forces political parties to be more circumspect and always to remain on standby mode. Controverting the contention that the two-party system does not usher in the open society, Popper cites instances how two major democracies (UK and USA) of the world have become an open society in spite of having the two-party system there. Distinguishing between political openness and cultural openness he holds that complete openness in the political front, like complete liberty, can backfire in the political arena.

An often-debated issue is whether in democratic governmental set-up representatives are merely a puppet in party's hand? Do they have the scope and capacity to apply their judgements? As far as scope is concerned, we have no qualms to say that it is extremely limited. However, the capacity issue is a controversial one and up for discussion. Another outstanding issue is whether they have the expertise to judge a complex societal issue. Exciting debates are on all these questions.

Thus, we can say that though the rallying cry of "government of the people, by the people, and for the people" has become a catchphrase, it gives us an only hazy picture of this political system. Is it not indeed paradoxical to think that if in this system ruler is people themselves, the distinction between the ruler and the ruled indeed becomes blurred? Do they not belong to two different classes? The interest of the ruling class and the ruled class can hardly converge. If it is "of the people" is it the majority's view that matters? We have seen that it is not always the case. We come to know that in a democracy maximum effort is given to protect the minority's views, interest; minority irrespective of any variables. Next, there is room for questioning: is it (i.e. government) for the people? Because a government that garners only a fragment of supports, as in more-than-two-party system, it might go on implementing its promises made during the election, though they have not got the endorsement of majority. Thus, the so-called legitimate laws are not grounded on Rousseau's "general will" of its people. D.D. Raphael makes the distinction between "agreement of all" and "interest of all". By making this distinction he held that in democracy majority views "should seek to serve the interests of all even though it does not have the agreement of all" (Popper 1988: 87). However, the moot question is: Is it indeed possible to serve the interest of all, given the fact that capability level and other factors make it virtually impossible to serve the interest of all? Is it not an unfeasible idea then? Though it might seem idealistic, to my mind there will always be a section of minorities whose views and interests will always be smothered. Taking a dig at the decision by the majority in democratic structure Amy Gutmann holds that it may be a theoretical requirement of democracy, but "it cannot be a sufficient democratic standard" (2012: 521).

As, in modern time, we hardly come across direct democracy and only representative democracy, in various forms, is widely practised, we can say that authorizing the representative to act in his/her favour is one essential feature of modern democracy. The system of recalling the representative even before completion of the term, if can be implemented, the scope of people's say can be increased but how much effective governance will it be is, of course, a moot question. There are some democracies, e.g. Ireland, where any amendment of the constitution needs to be placed before the public for endorsement through a referendum, whereas in many other democracies this is not a prerequisite. There were philosophers who did not prefer to transfer entire political authority of an individual to a representative. For example, Rousseau considered it noxious for democratic practice. In such a practice, individual imagines to be free only for a short period, i.e. during the election. Even in large democracy individual considers himself/herself insignificant as his/her well-considered and well-informed view may be nullified by ill-informed views of others. Once the election is over, he/she is again in the chain. It is indeed a fact that the inertia of people and not remaining vigilant, always gives tremendous scope to representatives to behave in a way he/she likes or to be enslaved by his/her party boss. Active participation in the political process, debate, watchfulness, etc.

keep always the representatives on their toe and also enhance an individual's competence in political affairs. Such enhancement of proficiency on political issues enables democratic governance to march effectively towards its goal. Such knowledge equips people in general with the required skill and information to make a good judgement even during choosing a representative. Without acquiring this skill, they are susceptible to choosing the wrong commissary. The very purpose of voting then may be self-defeating.

Another oft-cited feature of democracy is that it is a form of governance by discussion, persuasion and debate. D.D. Raphael holds that "discussion is an essential part of the democratic process" (Gutmann 2012: 91). Such discussions and persuasions render application of force useless. Hence, opposition parties and the common man can criticize the government's policies, persuade it to modify its views. Criticism of governmental policy by the opposition also persuades the electorate to see the flaws of the policy and wheedle electorates to choose them on the next occasion. This practice has been going on throughout the globe.

Separation of powers between different pillars of democracy, though not an essential condition, is practised in many democratic governments. It is this feature that sharply distinguishes it from other forms of governance such as monarchy. In non-democratic systems, there is a concentration of all powers at one place and hence it is susceptible to misuse, thereby restricting liberty and rights of its citizens. The process of separation of power had its origin in Europe and it was widely believed that, and as forcefully argued by the French judge of eighteenth-century, Montesquieu, such separation safeguards and extends liberty. Thus, in most democracies, we find the separation of the legislative function, executive responsibility and judicial activity. They work within their domain and by restricting one's encroachment into another's province there emerges some sort of checks and balances. The fourth estate, i.e. media, also plays a significant role in bringing forth the lacuna of either of these organs.

We saw before that the expansion of people's liberty and ensuring equality are two chief features of democracy. The concept of the universal franchise, which is in vogue at the modern time, exhibits the importance given to the notion of equality. As every adult citizen is allowed to cast his/her votes in elections, setting aside all other considerations such as level of education and other factors, it is assumed that everybody is treated as equal. One person–one vote–one value seems ideologically an excellent one. Despite its ideological merits, the debatable point is the rightness of the issue. The capability of all persons is not the same and hence decision/choice of less capable might overpower the more capable's choice. It is indeed a matter of concern. D.D. Raphael says that in modern-day democracy the idea that "a person is entitled to vote only if he or she has a reasonable measure of knowledge and education" (Gutmann 2012: 103) is repugnant to our leaders. This might sound elitism, however, there is a considerable substance in the view that practising democracy presupposes a decent level of universal education in force which effectively prepares everybody to raise him/her to a reasonable level. For practising democracy successfully, some groundwork is thus called for, so that a level-playing field is prepared for everybody's participation and the more capable or enlightened minds are not overshadowed by the less capable (not using the expression pejoratively). Perhaps, it is the opportunity of participation of all adult population of a country's election process that justifies its claim that democracy is a form of governance by the people and of the people. We do not find any significant further opportunity of participation in governance by the people as it is neither sought by rulers nor has viability.

Over time, modern democracies took significant steps to ensure human rights by ensuring certain freedoms which are usually considered as basic and constitutional rights as they are backed by legal protection. A philosophical analysis will show that the notion of human rights is actually a measure for ensuring certain liberties considered essential for a human being to live a dignified life. John

Locke contended that the principal aim of a government should be safeguarding natural rights of man. What constitutes natural rights is of course a moot point. For example, Locke in his conception of natural rights includes life, liberty and property. Though the third one, i.e. can the possession of property be part of natural rights, has generated a lot of debate. For example, Thomas Paine in his widely read book *The Rights of Man* (1791), written defending French Revolution against Edmund Burke's criticism of French Revolution in his *Reflections on the Revolution in France*, advocated property as a natural right of man as part of social security but the US Declaration of Independence did not mention this and rather replaced it with the pursuit of happiness. Rights to property, which was once a fundamental right in India, has been taken out later on.

In summing up the aforesaid points, we can say that among the political ideologies, democracy has many forms and variations which perhaps no other ideology known so far has. It appears that accepting this variation forms democracy's inner core. However, when the human mind tries to excavate some of its inner core or essence which, though appear to be elusive, still at least some of the following traits are present in the democratic political order. This is not to claim that all will be there as it is described, but some sort of family resemblance or criss-crossing will be noticed there. We can recount the following characteristics of democracy: Periodic elections, universal adult franchise, the existence of organized party system, independence of the judiciary, freedom of the press, etc. The periodic election in a fair manner at regular interval is a prerequisite for a democratic set-up for its people to choose their representative freely. Universal adult suffrage is found in most of the democracies though the definition of adulthood may be different in different countries. Here any discrimination on the basis of sex, caste, religion, wealth, race, etc. is denounced. It gives a feeling of empowerment to its people. Existence of political parties in modern democracy seems to be another essential condition. The number of parties may vary from country to country but the existence of a party system with clear ideology gives its people a scope to choose an alternative one if the present one fails to meet their expectations. Presence of a strong opposition party makes a democracy vibrant as the ruling party always remains vigilant lest the opposition is given a scope to enhance its popularity by pointing out its mistakes or better alternative. Existence of free press, also known as the Fourth Estate, is another requirement. It caters to the need of disseminating correct news and views which paves the way for the formation of public opinion. Separation of power enhances the freedom of people. Independence of the judiciary is the *sine qua non* for ensuring the rule of law and thwarting any misuse of the law. Various measures are taken to ensure the judiciary's independence. In addition to that, a constitution, written or unwritten, is another requirement. It limits the government by delineating rule of law and forestalling rule of someone's whims. Francis Graham Wilson (1936) in his *The Elements of Modern Politics: An Introduction to Political Science* holds that enunciation of some fundamental rights of people is another requirement of democracy.

Robert B. Talisse in his discussion of democracy distinguishes between the "schoolyard view" of democracy and the "aggregative views" of democracy (2013: 609). For him, the schoolyard view is a simple ilk of democracy and its chief characteristic is manifested in championing the liberal value of liberty and majority rule. These two traits, however attractive they may be, are highly abstract and demand further clarification. For instance, does one person–one vote is a sign of equality as usually it is claimed to be. Or, asks Talisse, should a requirement of equality demand that such a democratic process must

> take into account additional factors, such as the intensity or the order of individuals' preferences, or the informedness or rationality of individuals' votes, in order to treat members of the groups as equals.
> – Ibid.

Clubbing together modern democracies mostly flourished in the last century despite their variations he called them "aggregative view".

His interpretation of the aggregative view is akin to Rousseau's general will. As Talisse writes:

> The principle guiding the view is that when interests collide and yet a collective decision must be made, we should follow a procedure that affords to each actor equal input, and aggregates the inputs into a collective decision. Insofar as a collective decision is produced by a fair process that aggregates the preferences of all, it can be said to represent the popular will or common good. – 2013: 609

This view also contains in its womb the flaws of the schoolyard view as calculation of a bona-fide articulation of the majority will is indeed an almost impossible task. Citing Kenneth Arrow's view, Talisse writes:

> There is no way to transform expressions of individual preference into a rational collective decision that could possibly claim to represent the popular will. – Ibid.: 610

Thus, the notion of the popular will seems to be an elusive one. However, this should not lead us to conclude that democracy is not a practicable political order. In spite of its aforesaid unresolved issues, it is very much in practice and indeed a popular form of governance among all the available forms of governance.

In spite of apparent hollowness of the expression "popular will" thinkers made efforts to look at the issue from various angle to get hold of some of its common characteristics. Social scientists indeed were struggling for quite some time to find a way of happy combination between individual preferences, interests, etc. and collective decision. In the eighteenth century, Nicolas de Condorcet and Jean-Charles de Borda and later on in the nineteenth century Lewis Carroll developed the social choice theory in order to solve the above issue. Kenneth Arrow, a noted economist, in his 1951 book *Social Choice and Individual Values* and also Amartya Sen and some other thinkers later on applied that theory and popularized it in various fields. This is not to say that all of them gave the same theory. Rather, it is a family of models that shows us a path for aggregation of "individual inputs" for arriving at collective preferences. When applied to the popular will or common good in a democracy the question assumes the following shape: How can the aggregate arrive at a reasonable judgement/preference in selecting its representatives in spite of its members' individual judgements/interests? In brief, it provides us with a tool for studying collective decision-making method. Thus we find a way of collective decision making. The gap between individual and aggregate has thus been bridged.

William Riker in his *Liberalism Against Populism: A Confrontation Between the Theory of Democracy and the Theory of Social Choice* (1982) employs the social choice theory in order to investigate the reasonableness of the theory of democracy concerning its many practical limitations. He looks at the system from a different angle. He is of the opinion that a democratic machinery is a tool for preventing rulers from acting arbitrarily, to remove rulers who have upset them. Thus, he urges not to see democracy as a popular rule rather as "an intermittent, sometimes random, even perverse, popular veto" (1982: 244). Elitists, who consider some people are better gifted and hence be given more authority than the average, though see the thing from a different perspective, still consider democracy as a method for deciding its ruler by means of the popular vote. Rulers, in turn, have to act up to their electors' choice, otherwise, they will have to face the wrath of their people in the next election. The pluralists again take another stance for whom power does not lie in offices of government rather its expanse is the entire society. In society, people form different groups with homogeneous interests and among many such groups with varied and conflicting interest constant negotiations are carried out by the government. Thus we find efforts from various quarters to give interpretations of democracy that try to get hold of its core and by and large they consider this system conducive for maintaining social balance in spite of having many conflicting interests and competing groups. In their interpretations, we can notice that their analysis veers mainly on the descriptive side of the system. However, political philosophy being a subfield of moral philosophy cannot remain content with the only descriptive study. Democracy is a political ideology. Hence in addition to its descriptive share, it must have normative aspects also. It is evident from a definition given by Frank Thakurdas in his *Essays in Political Theory* (1982: 40) where he says:

> [Ideology] is a type of theory which upholds a certain political system (in its broadest sense) and the values and ideals that sustain it, as the final approximation of the human mind to an ideal arrangement and, therefore, claiming this finality seeks to realize it.

This definition tells us that the normative aspect of the political ideology under discussion cannot be renounced. In order to have an optimal view of this ideology, its normative aspect such as its scope of liberty, providing equality of opportunity and dispensing justice should get due consideration. Many more such questions (such as a government having the mandate to rule if wages a war against another country but the majority of its people consider it an unjust war or done only to draw political mileage should they stop paying tax which will be utilized for war-purpose) demand answers.

In addition to the above issue a question that arises in our mind is that as the democracy as a form of governance working for a quite long time — right from ancient Greece till date — how is it working and how are people satisfied. By and large, we can say that it is the most popular type of government and our statement is vouchsafed by the fact that electoral democracies grew by leaps and bounds in recent past. For example, from 1975 to 2005, we come to know that the number of countries practising electoral democracy swelled from 35 to 110. The triumph of Arab Spring that began with Tunisia and engulfed a large portion of Muslim countries, the collapse of Berlin Wall in 1989, disintegration of many communist countries such as the mighty USSR and many other such moves demonstrated the popularity and the admiration of pro-democratic trend. Francis Fukuyama, a social theorist of the West, once considered liberal democracy as the ultimate form of human government. He in his "The End of History?" says liberal democracy is "the end point of mankind's ideological evolution" and he predicted "universalization of Western liberal democracy as the final form of government" (1989: 4). He later reiterated this in his celebrated book *The End of History and the Last Man* (1992). There this social scientist showed how liberal democracy attracted people and who considered it a preferable system since the triumph of the French Revolution than any other available option. There was a debate about whether Fukuyama glorified only liberal democracy practised in the United States of America as a just political system or any form of parliamentary democracy. Scholars lean towards the latter view. His view has been commended as well as criticized. For example, in his *Specters of Marx: The State of the Debt, the Work of Mourning and the New International*, Jacques Derrida (1994) finds it as a sign of right-wing view that is sickening with cultural anxiety and is insistent on setting the seal on the death of Karl Marx. He also termed Fukuyama's view as virtually a Christian trend of describing finality. Derrida decries Fukuyama's attempt to describe liberalism as an ideology that has consummated as the only ideal in mankind's history. This is like prophesying the "end of ideologies" and this angered Derrida. For him, under this liberal democracy (even admitting its many appreciable characters) there is no gainsaying the fact that so many human beings have been "subjugated, starved or exterminated" and are subjected to various types of sufferings. Under this system, violence, economic oppression, inequality, famine, exclusion and innumerable forms of visible and invisible sufferings are vivid that we found never before. In such a situation, we cannot imagine the end of emancipatory discourses coming to an end.

The term "end" at "The End of History?" is susceptible to many interpretations. By using the term Fukuyama did not intend to mean that the era of human conflict is over; rather, he meant that ideological goal is best answered by liberal democracy and it is hardly possible to excel its central principles. In holding this he had in mind its rival principles found in communist ideas though later on, we find him balancing his view by underscoring the importance of communist ideology that once fell from grace due to multifarious factors out of which the identity issue stands out clearly. Adopting the term *thymos* from Socrates he showed that recognition for moral equality is so dominant in a human being that it surpasses many other cravings and this appetite can best be fulfilled by philosophical principles found in a liberal democracy.

Fukuyama observed many sparse incidents in between that did not signal the progressive rather regressive movement of liberal democracy such as the emergence of authoritarian government in some democratic countries and he termed these "democratic recessions". Even the authoritarian style of functioning by some democratic state was noticed by him and he firmly held that these are a type of test to evaluate concerned citizenry and how vibrant checks and balances of its democratic apparatus. The democratic mechanism has the strength within it to subdue such tyrants. It seems that his view about such deviation was almost like intermittent "market correction", an expression popular in economic activity.

In contemporary age, the political system is witnessing a struggle for an indomitable desire for recognition. Fukuyama in his book *Identity: The Demand for Dignity and the Politics of Resentment* (2018) traces the rise and progression of this identity politics, its fallout on politics that makes inroads in riving politics, and how this sentiment is posing threat to liberal democracy. He talks about two types of *thymos*: isothymia and megalotthymia. The former is the want to be seen equals with others and the latter is the hankering for "to be seen as superior". He considers these desires to be detrimental for democracy still he is of the opinion that fulfilment of these yearnings does not bring an end to the thirst of equal recognition, rather it might invigorate it. This identity yearning either on the basis of gender, political groups, or religion, on the one hand, unites people into groups, on the other, divide between groups. There is an inherent problem in identifying solely with people like him/her. This identity longing has been a bane for political left and boon for angry nationalism. This trend is fraught with danger, warns Fukuyama. His prescription was to ease this division by way of making more capacious groups. Such a measure will help in minimizing polarization.

In the recent past we find this political scientist worrying about "powerful elite" manipulating the political system by making use of money and muscle and thereby tilting electoral results in their favour. For him, it is a sign of decay in the system as it subverts popular will. In order to put a check on such decay, he now calls for resumption of left-wing political action. By holding this is he contradicting his "endism" stance taken previously or is he considering it only as instrumental for correcting syndromes of parliamentary democracy is indeed an intriguing inquiry.

References

Arrow, Kenneth, 1951, *Social Choice and Individual Values*, New York: John Wiley & Sons.

Derrida, Jacques, 1994, *Specters of Marx: The State of the Debt, the Work of Mourning and the New International*, New York/London: Routledge.

Ehrenberg, Victor, 1950, "Origins of Democracy", *Historia: Zeitschrift fur Alte Geschichte*, Bd. 1, H. 4 (*Source:* https://www.jstor.org/stable/4434319, accessed on 29 February 2020 at 09:03:09 UTC.)

Fukuyama, Francis, 1989, "The End of History?", in *The National Interest*, Summer, No. 16. (*Source*: https://www.jstor.org/stable/ 24027184 accessed on 17 June 2020.)

———, 1992, *The End of History and the Last Man*, New York: The Free Press.

———, 2018, *Identity: The Demand for Dignity and the Politics of Resentment*, New York: Farrar, Straus, and Giroux.

Gutmann, Amy, 2012, "Democracy", in *A Companion to Contemporary Political Philosophy*, ed. R.E. Goodin et al., 2nd edn, Oxford: Wiley-Blackwell.

Mandela, Nelson, 1994, *Long Walk to Freedom*, Boston, MA: Little, Brown and Co.

Miller, David, 2003, *Political Philosophy: A Very Short Introduction*, Oxford: Oxford University Press.

Paine, T., 1791, *Rights of Man*, London: J.S. Jordan.

Popper, Karl, 1988, *The Open Society and Its Enemies Revisited.* (*Source:* https://www.economist.co/democracy-in-america/2016/01/31/from-the-archives-the-open-society-and-its-enemies-revisited accessed in July 2020.)

Raphael, D.D., 2009, *Problems of Political Philosophy*, 2nd edn, New York: Palgrave Macmillan.

Rawls, John, 1971, *A Theory of Justice*, Cambridge, MA: Harvard University Press.

Riker, W., 1982, *Liberalism Against Populism: A Confrontation Between the Theory of Democracy and the Theory of Social Choice*, New York: W.H. Freeman and Co.

Schumpeter, A.S., 1943, *Capitalism, Socialism and Democracy*, London: George Allen & Unwin.

Sivaramakrishnan, A., 2017, *Introduction to Political Ideologies: Contexts, Ideas, and Practices*, New Delhi: Sage Publications.

Suu Kyi, Aung San, 1991, *Freedom from Fear*, ed. Michael Aris, New York: Penguin Books.

Talissse, R.B., 2013, "Democracy", in *The Routledge Companion to Social and Political Philosophy*, ed. Gerald Gaus and Fred D'Agostino, New York: Routledge.

Thakurdas, Frank, 1982, *Essays in Political Theory*, New Delhi: Gitanjali Publishing House.

Wilson, Francis Graham, 1936, *The Elements of Modern Politics: An Introduction to Political Science*, New York: McGraw-Hill.

2

On Infringement upon Democratic Rights

Kausik Bhattacharya

I

THE concept of democracy incorporates the idea of a citizen having certain rights which are called democratic rights. Various instruments of the state are supposed to ensure people's democratic rights. There are also instruments of the state that are entrusted for providing relief to the people if their democratic right is infringed.

An ideal democratic state is that where infringement upon people's democratic right seldom occurs, and whenever occurs people get quick relief. Such an ideal situation may prevail not only due to the efficiency, honesty and integrity of the people involved in administration but also due to the quality of the non-administrative people who do not usually involve themselves in infringement of other people's democratic right. It follows that quality of the people or human resources of the state is an important factor in respect of maintaining democratic atmosphere in the state.

A less ideal situation is that where infringement of people's democratic right often occurs, but people get quick relief either due to the efficiency of the administration or due to the efficiency of the judiciary.

A further less ideal situation involves frequent violation of people's democratic right lacking administrative or judicial relief. Administration and the ruling party become corrupt. Often administration itself, in collaboration with a political party, destroys people's democratic right, and judiciary becomes corrupt. Media gives up its impartial nature. Under these circumstances, people may cast their vote against the ruling party to form a new government.

The situation becomes bad when people cannot express their opinion freely and cast their vote against a political party due to political terrorism, and it becomes worst when people find no better alternative as they find all the political parties as equally corrupt and rotten.

II

What indicates whether the democratic atmosphere of a state is good, bad or worst is which political issues are important to the people. In a dying democracy, negative issues like corruption and political terrorism get more importance than the economic policy, the policy for the development of the country, etc. in an election. The reason for this is as follows.

People will be interested in making a comparison between two different economic or developmental policies adopted by two different political parties and choose one only if they have the confidence that the economic or developmental policy would be implemented with honesty and integrity. But too much corruption diverts the funds from development and consequently the economic or developmental policy which has been adopted becomes immaterial. Again, too much political terrorism destroys the social security of people, and when the existence of people is at stake, the issue as to which economic policy would be adopted becomes less important.

In an advanced democracy, a negative issue like corruption or political terrorism rarely becomes the main issue in the political field, and when it becomes an issue the political career of the person concerned is ruined. Compared to scams and scandals we find in India, the Watergate scandal of political spying in the US is virtually nothing, still it destroyed the political career of President Nixon. This is because of the quality and mature political consciousness of a vast majority of the people belonging to an advanced democratic state. A person involved in scam will lose the support of almost all the people as they are all united against basic threats to democracy. In an advanced democratic state, most of the people are not committed to any political person or party. Existence of less number of committed voters is a mark of advanced democracy.

III

I have already indicated that in a decayed democracy people face political terrorism if they express their opinion against a political party or intend to cast their vote against a political party, and it is the presence of a high percentage of committed voters is one of the important factors that invites political terrorism which force some people to cast their vote in favour of a particular political party and prevents some people to cast their vote against the political party. Let us see how the presence of high percentage of committed voters creates the scope for political terrorism. Suppose a very high percentage of non-committed voters exists in a state. It is difficult for a political party to terrorize a high percentage of voters in order to secure the required number of votes for winning an election. Moreover, the act of terrorization will antagonize almost all the voters. But if a political party has, say, 35 per cent committed voters, it becomes relatively easy for a political party to achieve the required number of votes by terrorizing a relatively small number of voters, say, 10 or 15 per cent.

The above scenario may give the impression that the development of a particular type of political consciousness resulting in withdrawal of commitment of a large number of voters towards any political party and their unity on some basic issues may create a better political atmosphere. But the situation is not so simple. Consider the worst situation we have described earlier where all the political parties are equally corrupt and involved in power struggle by employing violence and promoting political terrorism causing infringement of people's democratic rights. In this situation withdrawal of mass support from a political party will not improve the situation if people have no other alternative or option but to support some other political party having more or less equal status.

In view of the above, the Hon'ble Supreme Court of India allowed the voters to exercise "no choice" or "none of the above" option in an election if they are of the opinion that none of the contesting candidates is suitable. Still the exercise of "no choice" option will not prevent an unsuitable candidate from being elected unless there is law or rule stating that, if the majority of the voters exercise the "no choice" option, a re-election will take place involving entirely fresh candidates. People, who intend to protect the democratic atmosphere in the state, may initiate a movement to force the legislation to frame such a law.

Even if the above-mentioned law comes into force, the situation will not be improved unless the majority of the voters exercise "no choice" or "none found suitable" option whenever the objective situation demands. And whether in an appropriate situation majority of the people will exercise "no choice" or "none found suitable" option or not depends upon the understanding, education and political conscious of people belonging to the state. It is the quality of the people of the state that ultimately determines the democratic atmosphere of the country.

Before blaming the political leader, administration and judiciary, and making them responsible for the death of democracy, we should blame ourselves. Our politicians, administration and judiciary would just like be the same as what we are and do the same thing in wider sphere as we do in a limited sphere in our family, society and work place.

IV

In a dying or dead democracy, where almost all the political parties are involved in corruption and power struggle by employing violence and promoting political terrorism, replacement of one political party by another in an election is not a fruitful solution. Rather, without showing commitment to any political party we should take such a measure that will force all the political parties to improve themselves in a fair competition.

The paradox of democracy is that we elect the authority to protect our freedom and democratic right, but the authority once elected may destroy our freedom and put an end to democracy. That is why Karl Popper, while criticizing the Marxist, held the view that the fundamental problem of all politics is the control of all controllers, of checking the dangerous accumulation of power represented in the state. We may replace the bad rulers to have good rulers, but experience shows us that we are not likely to get them. Even the best man may be corrupted by the power. Thus, it is important to design our institutions in such a way that these institutions prevent bad rulers from causing too much damage. Establishment of a law or rule stating that, if the majority of the voters exercise the "no choice" option, a re-election will take place involving entirely fresh candidates, may be a step towards the achievement of this end.

V

I shall conclude this essay with a few words on our commitment towards a political party. Many of us usually do not withdraw our commitment towards a political party unless we are directly and personally affected by the policies and the activities of that party. We remain indifferent when the policies and activities of government formed by elected members of that party interfere with the democratic rights of the others. For instance, most of us remain indifferent when a policy of the government interferes with the democratic rights of the tribes and destroys their social security. The oppression of the minority invites terrorism and terrorism, in turn, destroys our democratic rights, for instance, the right to life.

If a bomb blast takes the life of a member of our society, we accuse the terrorists for killing an innocent person, but we forget that it is the oppression of the government elected by us gave rise to terrorism, and that we have a responsibility to prevent the government from oppressing the minority and to protect the democratic rights of the minority. We should not forget that democracy is not majority rule, and that, if a single citizen of the state remains socially unsecured, none of the rest can remain socially secured.

3

Kauṭilya and His Arthaśāstra

A Notion of Democracy in Ancient Indian Society

Projit Kumar Palit

Introduction

THE genesis history of Indian democracy is rooted from Indian political and dhārmic (religious) thought from Vedic philosophy. So, in early Indian society, democratic thought and humanist religiosity were deeply linked with Indian philosophy and both were complementary to each other (Palit 2012: 15). It has occupied a great place in the corpus of knowledge of the ancient Indian civilization. The Indian democracy cannot be examined, interpreted and translated without the help of *dharma* (religion) and its values (ibid.). In Vedic period, democracy was appeared the forms of *sabhā*s and *samitis* (Palit 2008: 80). There is no doubt that both institutions enjoyed a high prestige in Vedic age like the modern parliament. The *Atharvaveda* described that *sabhā*s and *samiti*s as the twin daughters of Prajāpati, the creator (ibid.: 81). The average state of the Ṛgvedic period consisted of only a few square miles like the city state of ancient Greece. It had a capital, not much larger that a few dozen villages comprised in it (ibid.: 89). Villages had their own popular assemblies known as *sabhā*s and the capital had the central assembly for the whole state, which was called a *samiti*. In the Vedic age, title of the kings was varying from region to region. King of Madhyadeśa was designated *rājā*, the chief of the western region was *samrāṭ*, of northern *virāṭ* and of the southern *bhoja*. The differences in titles were used by the kings from region to region but the presence of the *sabhā* and *samiti*s like the council of ministers was common to all (ibid.: 89-91). Though, this concept was not only the subject matter of the Greek society but also had seen in Indian scenario during much early period. Vedic democracy is the foundation of Kauṭilya's state concept. So Kauṭilya tried to develop a welfare state which consisted of legal equality, freedom and rule of law (Rangarajan 1992: 45-49). His democracy was based on welfare and it provided to the citizens the quality of life, dignity, freedom, and a healthy and happy living society. Kauṭilya's *Arthaśāstra* is still the foundation of political and social thoughts of the Indian society. It is also the code book of the economic and administrative schemes of a sovereign state. Kauṭilya thought that human beings were the real capital of any nation. So, the citizens of the nation were powerful which means good deployment of the family and nation (ibid.: 67-68).

Kauṭilya and His Works

The *Manusmṛti* and Kauṭilya's *Arthaśāstra* were the first two authentic books of ancient India that elaborately describe different theories about state formation and the concept of democracy. Kauṭilya was also known as Viṣṇugupta or Cāṇakya. It is argued that as he was born in "Kuṭala gotra", he came to be known as Kauṭilya (Bhattacharjee 2019: 34). This highly learned brāhmaṇa at first served the Nanda king of Magadha, a place that presently lies in Bihar. But later on he was insulted by Dhanānanda, and he left the Nandas. Ultimately, Candragupta and Kauṭilya together attacked Magadha and defeated Dhanānanda in 323 BCE. It is a fact that Candragupta could establish a large and mighty empire only under the able guidance of Kauṭilya (Mazumder 2010: 21-15).

Kauṭilya was a great philosopher and minister during 317–293 BCE in Candragupta Maurya's kingdom. His knowledge ranged from statecraft, politics, diplomacy, war, ethics, among others. During his period, he was considered as the shrewdest, and he advocated his king in accounting and financial management (Chandrasekaran 2006: 8-12). The *Arthaśāstra's* coverage includes economics, political science, public administration, law and statecraft (Thapar 1966: 27). It was intended to provide practical advice for the management of the state and thereby enhance the wealth of the nation (Kosambi 1965: 41). Kauṭilya was also famous for his two other works: the *Cāṇakyasūtras* and *Cāṇakya-Rājanītiśāstra*. In each of these works he emphasized on accounting and financial regulations (Sihag 2008: 127).

The *Cāṇakyasūtras* dealt with the rules of science and *Cāṇakya-Rājanītiśāstra* emphasized on the science of government and policy science; all three works of Kauṭilya were embossed on four major factors:

i. development of accounting principles,
ii. requirement of accounting methodology and scope,
iii. codification of regulations and rules of accounting along with designing the organizational structure aimed at reducing conflicts of interest, and
iv. control of fraudulent accounting, i.e. ethical accounting; pursuit of happiness; efficient resource allocation and upholding law and order (Chandrasekaran 2006: 129; Sihag 2016: 128).

Kauṭilya pointed out three factors through his works: first, his thinking pattern which was broad and strategic; second, his knowledge upon vast areas, such as ethics, economy, science, war, state, statecraft, diplomacy and social structure; and third, his works are quite apt for any modernized accounting/taxation system of states. The contributions made by the works of Kauṭilya not only dominated the ancient Indian tax system but also attracted the modern Indian philosophers and ministers to adopt the taxation regulations and its system to develop the country towards betterment. Kauṭilya's treatise is a deeply-rooted concept that changed Aśoka (Maurya's grandson) who adopted the *Arthaśāstra* and followed *dharma* by renouncing war and brutality, this made him a diplomatic emperor rather than an autocratic (Bhattacharjee 2019: 34-67).

The Characteristics of Kauṭilya's Arthaśāstra

Cāṇakya might have written the *Arthaśāstra* during 350–283 BCE, but it is uncertain that many authors and philosophers together created the *śāstra* from 250 BCE. Since the dates and authorships are unclear, it is presumed that the treatise created by aristocrats, philosophers and advocacies might have been combined into significant *śāstra*s, prior the *Arthaśāstra*. Though there are no validations for the given facts, it was argued by several scholars (Sury 1990: 67; Altekar 1992: 89) that "the *Arthaśāstra* was the primary source for accounting management and tax system". Conversely, it was found that, Kauṭilya was a Mauryan minister and hence it can be assumed that the *Arthaśāstra* should have been written in-between 350–283 BCE. During those periods, Sanskrit was the primary language used by scholars (Battacherjee 2019: 44-49).

The Kauṭilyan treatise was considered lost until Rudrapaṭnam Shamasastry, an Indian librarian, identified it in 1905. After the work got identified, many scholars and authors like Basham (1959), Boesche (2002) and Olivelle (2013) tried to understand it by translating it into their language. Shamasastry himself translated and published the treatise in English in 1915, in instalments, since the treatise was hard to translate (Nandi and Palit 2010: 12-13). According to J.F. Fleet,

> we are, and shall always remain, under a great obligation to him (Shamasastry) for a most important additions to our means of studying the general history of ancient India.
>
> – Quoted in Shamasastry 1961: 38-39

Before discovering the *Arthaśāstra* manuscript, Kauṭilya existed within the quotes of Manu, Uśanas, Bṛhaspati, Bharadwāja, Vātavyādhi, Viśālākṣa, Piśūna, Kaunapadanta, Parāśara and other scholars mentioned Kauṭilya thought and his words in their books (Rangarajan 1992: 89). Afterward, another two or three manuscripts of the *Arthaśāstra* were traced which helped further to study the various obscurities of the text (Nandi and Palit 2010: 12).

According to the *Arthaśāstra*, *artha* (purposes), *dharma* (ethical), *adharma* (unethical), *vārtā* (wealth), *nyāya* (justice), *anyāya* (unjust), *kāma* (pleasure/emotions), *mokṣa* (spiritual liberation) and *ānvikṣikī* (philosophy), *veda*, science of economics and government are the vital aspects that were found throughout the treatise (Kangle 2000: 89). Majorly, the treatise comprised of rules and regulations, political aspects, accounting laws, rules on wars, socio-economical activities, tax system, human rights, etc. Hence, the *Arthaśāstra* was not only a powerful treatise but also a strategic and broad piece of work suggesting to alter the socio-economic development of a state, when rightly implemented. In brief:

> *artha-evapradhānaḥ artha-mūlau dharma-kāmau ...*
>
> *artha* (purpose) paves its way for *dharma* (justice); whereas *dharma* and *kāma* (emotions/lust) rely on *artha*. So, overall, without a purpose, there is neither justice nor emotions that would pave the way for *mokṣa* (divinity). – Mishra 2016: 78

Kauṭilya's Arthaśāstra and Root of Indian Democracy

The significance of the *Arthaśāstra* in Indian history:

a. The original state of anarchy and the origin of the king and government.

b. The concept of the state, *prakṛtis*, the territorial divisions, etc.

c. Various forms of government – republican and monarchial.

d. Popular assemblies in monarchy – limits king's authority.

e. Royal consecration and powers of king and feudatories.

f. Public administration, and designation and functions of administrative officers.

g. Public finance, various forms of revenue, principles of taxation, tolls and levies, pay and emoluments.

h. Judicial administration – civil, criminal and personal laws, police, espionage.

i. Foreign policy, functions of emissaries.

j. Principles of aggression, treaty and neutrality.

k. Military organization.

The form of the work is said to be the combination of *sūtras* and *bhāṣya* (Bhattacharjee 2019: 62).

Kauṭilya's *Arthaśāstra* refers to Manu, Uśanas, Bṛhaspati Bharadwāja, Vātavyādhi, Viśālākṣa, Ambhīyas, Kātyāyana, Dīrghacyavana, Ghotamukha, Kiñjalka, Piśūnaputra and others. Five different schools of political thought – those of Bṛhaspati, Uśanas, Pracetas Manu, Parāśara and Ambhi – are mentioned by him, including his own opinions on their theories (Bhattacharjee 2019: 105-20). Evidently, Kauṭilya did not start any new system of governance, but he did begin a new direction in political thought of Realism. Roger Boesche in his book on Kauṭilya calls him "The first great political realist". He made a clear distinction between religion and politics, and did not evaluate political problems in terms of religious thought. He urged that history was not the outcome of the vengeance of the supernatural but the expression of human intelligence. A supporter of benevolent monarchy, Kauṭilya stressed on discipline and honesty as basic requisites of material and spiritual progress, the goals of society (Bhattacharjee 2019: 115-16). He wanted the king to speed up the moral and material welfare of his subjects by properly constituted administrative machinery. *Daṇḍa* (royal sceptre) was needed to inflict strong punishments on criminals, traitors and anti-socials. With its help, the king must arrest any anarchy in the state and ensure smooth working of administration. Kauṭilya is easily one of the most famous

Indian political thinkers who participated in the social and political revolutions of his age for collective welfare of the common man. He visualized an empire that was well-knit, prosperous, secular, crime-free and built on the timeless Vedic tenets of harmony, equality, compassion and honesty. Kauṭilya believed that people, among whom the bounds of the Aryan rule of life are fixed, among whom the *varṇas* and the stages of life are securely established and who are guarded by the three Vedas, prosper, do not perish. He identified the necessary requisites for this; a sound code of civil and criminal law, an impartial judiciary, liberal private property rights, strong infrastructure, incentive mechanisms to ensure efficient and honest officials, and a faithful military. The *Kauṭilīya Arthaśāstra* contains his profound insights on this power index of growth and well-being. *Artha* is regarded as one of the *trivarga* (three goals of human existence), the other two being *dharma* and *kāma*. *Artha* is the substance or livelihood (*vṛttiḥ*) of men; in other words, it means "the earth inhabited by men". "*Arthaśāstra* is the science which is the means of the acquisition and protection of the earth." Thus, in his first *sūtra*, Kauṭilya says:

> This single (treatise of the) science of politics has been prepared mostly by bringing together (the teaching of) as many treatises on the science of politics as have been composed by ancient teachers for the acquisition and protection of the earth.

The *Kauṭilīya Arthaśāstra* seeks the means for the overall well-being which was possible only through the assistance of the state. Hence, adhering to the tenets of the *Arthaśāstra* became the most essential function of statecraft. Besides promoting the welfare of the portion of the earth in its jurisdiction and safeguarding its inhabitants, the acquisition of new territory and protection of this acquired population also became the king's duty (Bhattacharjee 2019: 109-12). Thus, the *Arthaśāstra* deals with state affairs in the internal as well as in the external spheres, i.e. it encompasses politics, sociology, administration and justice, crime and punishment, defence, offence and warfare strategies, espionage and counter-espionage network in a categorical and authoritative manner.

Many writers like Manu, Bṛhaspati, Nārada and Parāśara had dealt with *artha-nīti* (socio-economic policy), *daṇḍa-nīti* (judicial system and politics) and *videśa-nīti* (foreign policy) before Kauṭilya. They deserve praise for their efforts but it was Kauṭilya who developed a purposeful and comprehensive framework of guidelines of good governance.

Despite deliberating extensively on polity and statecraft, Kauṭilya, in his *Arthaśāstra*, has not mentioned a single event contemporaneous to himself or his protégé, Candragupta. It appears, therefore, that the principles of diplomacy and kingship he laid down were for the use of rulers in general, not of any particular community. It is also possible that he penned down these theories much before his active political life, may be at Taxila when he taught at the university there.

The *Arthaśāstra* sought to comprehend and enhance the whole economic and social life and externally it aimed at the sovereignty of the whole of India. The advanced technique of statecraft is evident from the fact that Kauṭilya directed the state officers to record the details of regions, villages, castes and families in voluminous registers. To Kauṭilya, sovereignty was inherent in the unity and organization of state. A staunch believer in the harmonious blending of might and wisdom, Kauṭilya proclaimed that the end of justice should be the happiness of the common man, who was the main prop of the state which was actuated by moral and ethical standards. Pursuing successful economic policies through productive enterprises was also needed to empower the state treasury (*koṣa*). A balance should, thus, be ensured between the welfare of the people and augmenting the resources of the state.

This would presuppose two things – maintenance of law and order, and adequate administrative machinery. Conquest and acquisition of new territory was also required to enhance the national exchequer. The safeguarding of existing territory from enemies, both within and without, was also vital (Bhattacharjee 2019: 131-42). Viṣṇugupta or Cāṇakya or Kauṭilya commonly known among the people as Kauṭilya or Cāṇakya, changed the views of taxation through his *Arthaśāstra* treatise. The term *artha* projects "purpose" or "meaning" and *śāstra* derived from Sanskrit (*śāstra*) which means "science" or "rule"; together *Arthaśāstra* defines one's life and the purpose of life (Bhattacharjee 2019: 149-52). Kauṭilya was the minister of Candragupta Maurya; it is assumed that during his reign, Kauṭilya created the *Arthaśāstra*, aimed at sustaining the belief of the king's subjects and the emperor's expectations. The treatise comprises of fifteen books, 150 chapters and 180 topics. The *Arthaśāstra*'s fifteen books and their break-up of chapters and topics are given in Table 3.1.

Table 3.1: Books, Chapters and Topics in the Arthaśāstra*

	Book Title	*Chapters*	*No. of Topics*
1.	Training	21	1 to 18
2.	Superintendent's activities	36	19 to 56
3.	Justice	20	57 to 75
4.	Eradication of thorns	13	76 to 88
5.	Secret conduct	6	89 to 95
6.	The circle's basis	2	96 to 97
7.	Sixfold strategy	18	98 to 126
8.	Calamities	5	127 to 134
9.	King's activity and preparations for marching into a battle	7	135 to 146
10.	War	6	147 to 159
11.	Confederacy conducts	1	160 to 161
12.	Weaker king	5	162 to 170
13.	Techniques of confining a fort		171 to 176
14.	Esoteric practices	4	177 to 179
15.	Scientific treatise's organization		179 to 180

* *Source*: Shamasastry 1956.

Kauṭilya details how was the king responsible to the state and its people, and how should he follow the rules and regulations of the state as a citizen. According to the *Arthaśāstra*, a good empire or king should always introduce fair and justified taxation in his state, he should be ethical and open-minded. The *Arthaśāstra* defines that a king should rather be loyal to his people than taxing more than their capacity, which would not only be unjust, but also it would devastate the wealth of the empire (Bhattacharjee 2019: 159-62).

Kauṭilya's Arthaśāstra and Indian Democracy

According to Kauṭilya, the source of livelihood of man is wealth and *Arthaśāstra* for a nation is the wealth in the form of both the territory of the state and its inhabitants with a variety of occupations. No wonder, the scripture also prescribes measures to protect this wealth from various calamities, natural as well as man-made. It places a great emphasis on the welfare of the people and dictates ethics and morality of urban living. Through a number of verses, the *Arthaśāstra* also dictates measures for environmental protection and animal welfare.

The treatise is a masterpiece of statecraft, politics, military warfare, law, accounting systems, taxation, fiscal policies, civil rules, internal and foreign trade, etc. Subjects including medicine, gemology, metallurgy, measures of length, tables of weights, divisions of time, etc. are also highlighted along with many others. Often referred to as a guide to political sciences and fundamentals of management, the treatise also throws light on the evolution of urban studies in ancient India. Although less has been explored in this direction, it provides an insight into assessing and enhancing the capacities of the states in managing the adverse and disastrous situations due to natural or manmade reasons.

The *Arthaśāstra* scientifically conducts surveys on the agriculture, forestry, methods of elephant taming and training, horse training, mining and so on. The *Arthaśāstra* manuscript is a remarkable episode in the academic history of India because it provides new interpretations to public administration, welfare, democracy, the duties of the king, ministers and officials and the art of diplomacy and statecraft. The happiness of any king is identified with the happiness of his subjects. This is the main objective of the *Arthaśāstra*.

The *Arthaśāstra* literally means "scripture of wealth" but it is a highly philosophical book of administration of the state. Kauṭilya divided societies based on the size of population and availability of the economic resources and development (Deshkar 2014: 87-95). The smallest division was a village which was formed within 100 farmer families and bigger was not extended more than 500 families. Kauṭilya also emphasized the quality of life of society and its various developmental works.

Kauṭilya adopted the "clusters approach" administration and he divided the state into more than ten clusters and each cluster consisted of certain number of villages. One cluster of around 800 villages was to be centred by a *sthānīya* (a fortress of that name), 400 villages by a *droṇamukha*, 200 villages by a *khārvātika* and a *saṅgrahaṇa* in the midst of ten villages (Deshkar 2014: 89-95). These centres acted as town halls or probably like the hierarchical local governing authorities supporting the administrative functioning of the state. Games and sports were not allowed in the village. Not only that various performers of society like drummers, dancers and clowns were not allowed in villages because they might disturb the life of village people who were the real work-force (Deshkar 2014: 90-95). But land was allotted outside the villages for games, sports and other amusements.

Kauṭilya gave first priority to the utilization of land and the natural resources like forests, soils, rivers, water, minerals, etc. He divided the land into various sectors, depending upon the productivity of soil. Kauṭilya specified the type of plantations for each category of land. He allotted the forest land for planting delicious fruit trees, bushes, bowers and thornless trees for animate or inanimate objects.

Kauṭilya also classified (Rangarajan 1992: 162) the whole land based on rainfall such as

- Crown land
- Private land
- Forests
- Pastures
- Elephant forests
- Reserved for ascetics
- Wildlife sanctuaries
- Reservoirs
- Crown property
- Private property
- Mines
- Land suitable for settlement
- Wasteland

He selected the uncultivable land as pasture grounds. The countryside villages' lands were generally used for agriculture (Balkundi 2007: 27-29). The frontier regions of the state were marked with elephant forests and untamed jungles. The forts were built especially on the trade routes and other countries' side for protection. The tribes traditionally inhabited in jungles and they enjoyed certain special rights (Deshkar 2014: 91-95). They were not completely controlled by the state. Thus, it seems that the tradition of making keen observations on various aspects of crop cultivation must have continued since long before Kauṭilya (Balkundi 2007: 27). Kauṭilya tried to develop scientific farming, forestry, specified the duties and responsibilities of different *adhyakṣas*, e.g. the superintendent of agriculture, superintendent of cows or horses or elephants and he developed a scientific knowledge system through observation and empirical studies. This has been established scientifically that the genesis of agricultural practice in India can be traced back to a period around 7000 BCE (Shamasastry 1961: 38-42). Indian agricultural knowledge reached a level of development and agricultural science took a definite shape in *circa* third century BCE. Kauṭilya specified the required qualification of the superintendent of agriculture in the *Arthaśāstra* (Shamasastry 1961: 89). According to him, the superintendent of agriculture had to be a person who was highly experienced and knowledgeable in the disciplines of agronomy, horticulture, and plantation of bushes and trees; he had to collect seeds of all kinds of grains, flowers, fruits, vegetables, bulbous roots, fruits of creepers and cotton (ibid.: 127, *sūtra* 2.24.1). The *Arthaśāstra* also deals with the rainfall and soil classification. The relevant *sūtra* runs thus "the quantity of rain that falls in the country of Jungala is 16 *droṇas*; half as much more in moist countries, i.e. Anupa region; as the countries which are fit for agriculture (*deśavapanam*; 13½ *droṇas* in the country of Asmakas; 23 *droṇas* in Avantī and an immense quantity in western countries (*aparāntanam*), the boarders of the Himalayas and the countries where water channels are made for use in agriculture (*kulyavapaṇam*) (ibid.: 127, *sūtra* 2.24.4). Thus, it seems that the tradition of making keen observations on various aspects of crop cultivation must have continued since long before Kauṭilya. By the time of Kauṭilya, forecasting on rainfall based on planetary movements and related phenomena was in practice. India has had a rich tradition in mathematics and astronomy and there were definite attempts on the part of the early Indian researchers to correlate rainfall with astronomical phenomena which in the opinion of Y.L. Nene may be described as "astrology-based-rain-forecast" model for predicting rainfall in a season (Nene 2002: 55). Due to economic growth and political stability of Kauṭilya's time in the Mauryan period (322–185 BCE), civil infrastructure in that society was developed so impressively (Majumdar 1927: 12). Kauṭilya developed a communication system as well as public wells, rest houses and other facilities for the common public. One of the earliest evidences of a systematic communication service using foot messengers is found during the reign of Candragupta Maurya (322–298 BCE) (Shamasastry 1961: 89). A communication service between the capital and the far-off provinces of the vast kingdom served the needs of intelligence gathering and collection of revenue data, where regular messengers, *dūtas* (emissaries) and pigeons were used for conveying the royal communiqué. Kauṭilya elaborates on it diligently. The first efficient system of police and criminal administration in Indian political history buttressed by an elaborate system of espionage was developed during the Mauryan period. This totally indigenous concept of the organization of criminal administration supported by a well-planned hierarchy of spies who were employed to keep an eye and report on the criminal and anti-government activities of the people was Kauṭilya's brainchild to help build a formidable empire that could ensure welfare and growth of its citizens. Kauṭilya recommends two types of secret service: one is *saṁsthā* – the establishment, where the agents are stationed in a single place, the headquarters (Datta Majumdar 2010: 56). The other is *sañcāras*: the rover agents who move from place to place as per the requirements of their individual assignments. These two categories were further subdivided into certain categories.

The *saṁsthās* (*Kauṭilīya Arthaśāstra* 1.11.2-20) are of five kinds:

I. The sharp pupil or apprentice reporting any suspicious or evil dealings to the *samāhartṛ* (minister of spies),

II. *udasthita* – a dissident monk made the centre of an intelligence network of similar monks,

III. *grahapatikāvyāñjana* – the spy posing as a farmer,

IV. *vaidehakāvyāñjana* – the trader at the centre of the spying network of traders, and

V. *tapasāvyañjana* – a bogus ascetic made a secret agent but posing as a great seer (*Kauṭilīya Arthaśāstra* 1.12.1-5).

The *sañcāras* contained five varieties (Datta Majumdar 2010: 56):

- *sattrin* – an orphan trained as agent.
- *tīkṣṇa* – an assassin who secretly liquidated all enemies of the state.

- *rasada* – a chemist and poison-giver.
- *bhikṣukī* – a brāhmaṇa nun who spies on the very families who trust and honour her. Heretical nuns were also similarly employed (*Kauṭilīya Arthaśāstra* 1.12.1-5). The nature and mode of work of these spies was elaborately outlined by Kauṭilya in the *Arthaśāstra.*
- *kapaṭika* or a sharp disciple who is a skilful person capable of guessing the mind of others (*Kauṭilīya Arthaśāstra* 1.11.2). Encouraging him with money and honour, the *samāhartṛ* would direct him to report at once any evil-doing or suspicious behaviour of any person he may notice (*Kauṭilīya Arthaśāstra* 1.11.3).

Kauṭilya's espionage is the edifice on which subsequent spying designs can be structured, a model for future generations to admire and emulate (Datta Majumdar 2010: 89). Presumably, our immense pride for this cultural heritage shall undoubtedly be honoured even by our strongest critic, and Kauṭilyan secret service shall imbibe confidence and credence to diplomacy and governance even in forthcoming years. Emperor Aśoka however devised a very efficient means of communication which helped his success in building a vast empire, using a combination of mail runners, horse couriers, pigeon carriers and camels for official communication. Common chariots called *dagana* were sometimes used as mail chariots in ancient India (Thapar 1995: 54). Kauṭilya strongly argued that the communication system of the state was one of the pillars of espionage system and its democracy. This was exemplary of how an efficiently operated communication system gave that much-needed fillip to effective governance and the extra edge to an aggressive ruler, even in the ancient times. A royal highway connected Taxila with Pāṭaliputra and terminated at Tāmralipti, the main port in the Ganges delta. On the western coast the major port of Bhṛgukaccha/Barygaza (modern Bharuch) was connected with the Ganges Valley via Ozene (Ujjain). From the Narmadā Valley, the routes went into north-western Deccan and continued along rivers flowing eastward to various parts of the peninsula (Datta Majunmar 2010: 67).

India has a maritime history dating back to 7,600 years ("Ancient India: Indus Valley Civilization" mnsu.edu). The first trade-dock is possible to have been built at Lothal around 2300 BCE during the Indus Valley Civilization, near the present-day Mangrol Harbour on the Gujarat coast. The *Ṛgveda* written around 1500 BCE mentions Varuṇa with the knowledge of the ocean routes and describes naval expeditions. The *Rāmāyaṇa* refers to Yavana Dvīpa and Suvarṇa Dvīpa (Java and Sumatra) and also to Lohta Sayara (Red Sea Indians), who were masters of the sea-borne trade with Europe, Asia and Africa. A compass (*matsya yantra*) was used for navigation in the fourth and fifth centuries (Deogawank 2014: 4). Kauṭilya thought that trade and trading were more important for the state economy. Without good economy, welfare state and a peaceful society was not possible. So, Kauṭilya first developed a strong naval system in the Mauryan empire (Kangle 2000). The *Arthaśāstra* provides the earliest reference to the shipping system in ancient India. Kauṭilya writes about the Board of Shipping and the Commissioner of Port who supervised sea traffic. The *Arthaśāstra* devotes a full chapter on the state department of waterways under *nāvādhyakṣa* (Kangle 2000: 98-102). In fact, the word navigation is derived from the Sanskrit word *navgath*. The Sanskrit, Buddhist literature and Jātaka stories and Saṅgam literature also describe the naval supremacy of India based on Kauṭilīya's *Arthaśāstra*. Manu lays down laws to govern commercial disputes with respect to sea-borne traffic. The *Brahmāṇḍa Purāṇa* describes the world map drawn on a flat surface (Deogawank 2014: 93-95). Sea lanes between India and neighbouring lands were the usual form of trade for many centuries, and were responsible for the widespread influence of Indian culture on other societies. Powerful navies included those of the Maurya, Sātavāhana, Gupta, Coḷa, Pāṇḍya and Vijayanagara empires (Indian Naval: Early History. Indiannavy.nic.in – Retrieved on 6 January 2012). Kauṭilya was the founder of maritime trade and land trade system to other states. Kauṭilyan thought, established the idea of law and power of justice in ancient India, is still relevant to the modern society. Kauṭilya was imbued with a high social conscience. Kauṭilyan labour law, constitutional and administrative law, the law of commercial transactions, family law, international law, civil law and many other legal thoughts are still applied in India and Pakistan.

References

Altekar, A.S., 1992, *State and Government in Ancient India*, Delhi: Motilal Banarsidass.

Balkundi, H.V., 2007, "Placing the Period of Krishi Parashara", in *Glimpses of the Agricultural Heritage of India*, ed. Y.L. Nene, Secunderabad: Asian Agri-History Foundation.

Basham, A.L. (Arthur Llewellyn), 1959, *The Wonder that was India*, New York: Grove.

Bhattacharjee, Biman, 2019, "Tax System in Kauṭilya's Arthaśāstra", unpublished thesis, Assam University, Silchar.

Boesche, Roger, 2002, *The First Great Political Realist: Kautilya and His Arthashastra,* Lanham: Lexington Books.

Chandrasekaran, P., 2006, *Kauṭilya: Politics, Ethics and Statecraft*, Germany: University Library of Munich, MPRA Paper.

Datta Majumdar, Shilpi, 2010, "Concept of Espionage in Kautilya Arthaśāstra: Its Relevance to Present Era", unpublished thesis, Department of Sanskrit, Assam University.

Deogawank, Sangeeta, 2014, "History of Postal Communications in India, Ancient India, Part. http://www.hinduonnet.com/thehindu/2003/05/29/stories/2003052904851200.htm

Deshkar, Sameer M., 2014, "Kautilya Arthasastra and Its Relevance to Urban Planning Studies", *Institute of Town Planners, India Journal*, 7(1): 87-95.

Drekmeier, C., 1962, *Kingship and Community in Early India*, Stanford: Stanford University Press.

Kangle, R.P., 2000, *Kauṭilīya Arthaśāstra*, New Delhi: Oxford University Press.

Kosambi, D.D., 1965, *The Culture and Civilization of Ancient India in Historical Outline*, London: Routledge and Kegan Paul.

Majumdar, G.P., 1927, *Vanaspati: Plants and Plant Life as in Indian Treatises and Traditions*, Calcutta: University of Calcutta.

Majumdar, R.C., 2010, *Corporate Life in Ancient India*, Second edition, Calcutta: University of Calcutta.

Mishra, M., 2016, "Kauṭilya's Arthaśāstra: Restoring Its Rightful Place in the Field of International Relations", *Journal of Defence Studies*, 10(2): 77-109. http://idsa.in/jds/jds_10_2_2016_Kauṭilya-s-Arthasastra

Nandi, S.G. and Projit Kumar Palit, 2010, *Manuscript and Manuscriptology in India*, New Delhi: Kaveri Books.

Nene, Y.L., 2002, "*Modern Agronomic Concepts and Practices Evident in Kautilya's Arthasastra (c. 300 BC)*", *Asian Agri-History*, 6(3): 231-42.

Olivelle, Patrick, 2013, *King, Governance and Law in Ancient India: Kautilya's Arthaśāstra*, Oxford: Oxford University Press.

Palit, Projit Kumar, 2004, *History of Religion in Tripura*, New Delhi: Kaveri Books.

———, 2008, "Vedic Political System: Sabha and Samitees – An Early Parliamentarian Concept of India", *Journal of the Department of Sanskrit, Visva-Bharati*, 80-91.

———, 2012, "Indian Literature and Humanist Religiosity in Early Indian Society: A Historical Study", in *History in Literature: Literature as History*, ed. Priyadarsee Chakraborty, pp. 15-28, Kolkata: Levant Books and Kulti College.

Rangarajan, L.N., 1992, *Kauṭilya: The Arthasastra*, New Delhi: Penguin Books India.

Shamasastry, R. (tr.), 1956, *Chanakya's Land and Revenue Policy* (*Extracts of Arthasastra*) IA, 34: 5-10, 47-59, 110-19.

———, 1961, *Kauṭilya's Arthasastra*, Mysore: Mysore Printing and Publishing House.

Sharma, R.S., 2001, *Aspects of Political Ideas and Institutions in Ancient India*, Delhi: Motilal Banarsidass.

Sihag, B.S., 2008, "Kautilya on Risk-return Trade-off and Diversification", *Indian Journal of Economics and Business*, 7(2).

———, 2016, *Comparison of Kautilya's People-centric Approach to Machiavelli's King-centric Approach*, Mimeo.

Sury, M.M., 1990, "Tax Structure Developments in India: 1950-90, A Study on Indian Tax System", *Journal of Indian School of Political Economy*, 3(1): 1-37.

Thapar, Romila, 1966, *A History of India*, vol. 1, London: Penguin.

———, 1995, *Interpreting Early India*, Delhi: Oxford University Press.

Websites

- Ancient India. Indus Valley Civilization. mnsu.edu
- How to Build a Dock.Monsterguide.net (2009-06-15)
- http://prints.iiap.res.in/handle/2248/502
- http://www.archive.org/details/mghadtaorcloudm00wilsgoog

4

Problem of Democracy and Its Effects on Human Rights

Samar Kumar Mondal

Democracy

THE term "democracy" is very well known to all of us. It is an old concept. The concept of democracy had used not only in Greece but also in India. The ideal of democracy had spread out in many Indian religious scriptures, such as the *Rāmāyaṇa* and the *Mahābhārata*. The term *rāja-dharma* is usually used in terms of tenant's progress, welfare, benefit, etc. Though the term "democracy" is not mentioned in these scriptures, it is implicitly meant the ideals, which seek to explain by the term democracy. In *Mahābhārata* we get to see these ideals detailed and suggested to put in practice.

We have to mention here that the concept of democracy has flourished in the eighteenth and nineteenth centuries, because some developments like Industrial Revolution and Renaissance in Europe helped to spread it in the world. Similarly, fight for independence in the United States of America and the French Revolution also helped to the widespread acceptance of the concept of democracy.

Human beings have struggled to establish a particular type of ideal system, like democracy. Democracy is an old concept in politics. The term "democracy" arose from two Greek words, *demos*, which means people, and the other *kratos*, meaning rule or power (Yalf and Dautrich 2011: 6). All the forms of democracy are based to some extent on the original Greek notion of *dēmokratia*. That means "government by the people". The core concept of the term democracy is based on the freely expressed will of the people for determining their own political, social and cultural systems and their full participation in all aspects of their life. There are so many definitions of democracy and a particular definition is more correct to us which has been given by Abraham Lincoln.

According to him (1863), democracy is "government of the people, by the people, and for the people". Some thinkers believe that this definition is defective. They have given many reasons to support their opinions. Some thinkers who do not accept the definition of democracy given by Abraham Lincoln, are A.V. Dicey and Lord Bryce. Their opinion is that the definition of democracy is very straight. They argue that in "government of the people", the term "of the people" is indistinct. It may mean the direct rule of the people, it may mean the total population, it may mean the rule of majority and may also mean the rule of the people. According to Diecey and Bryce, it is not acceptable that democracy means the rule of all people. It is not imaginable that infants, mad people and traitors were participated in the election in any country. That is why Dicey defined democracy as a form of government in which the governing body is a comparatively large section of the entire society (Dicey 1961: 50). Lord Bryce also accepts this type of definition. According to him, in reality, democracy is a rule by majority.

> This means in communities which act by voting, the rule belongs to the majority, as no other method has been found for determining peaceably and legally what is to be declared the will of the community which is not unanimous". – 1962: 20

In democracy every member of a particular state plays a vital role in the selection of the government. In this system every person has equal right, that is why some thinkers say that democracy is a government conducted by every person or citizen.

Liberalism

Most political philosophers have sought to justify coercive institutions; they have simply disagreed over what sort of coercive institutions are justified. Liberalism, which derives from the work of John Locke, is of the view that coercive institutions are justified when they promote liberty. According to John Locke, liberty requires a constitutional monarchy with a parliamentary system of government.

> He insists that each and every individual grants his whole liberty to the supreme legislative power, which is a necessary mark of all civil societies, and is the representative of all. – Laslett 1960: 20

Over time, however, the ideal of liberty got at least two interpretations. The first libertarianism, the view that seems closest to that of Locke is classical liberalism, which is now more frequently called interpreters' constraints on liberty as positive acts. In contrast, the second welfare liberalism, a form of liberalism derived from the work of T.H. Green (1999: 7), in interpreted to include the limitation on freedom, also negative actions that prevent people from doing what they might otherwise do. According to this view, failing to help people in need does restrict their liberty. He argues that even though the state has no intrinsic value, its intervention in society is necessary to provide the conditions that enable rational beings to achieve self-satisfaction.

Both libertarianism and welfare liberalism are committed to individualism. This view takes the rights of individuals to be basic and justifiers the actions of coercive institutions as promoting those rights. On the other hand, common libertarianism, which derives from the writings of Georg Wilhelm Friedrich Hegel, rejects individualism. It maintains that rights of individuals are not basic and that the collective can have rights that are independent of and even opposed to what liberals claim as the rights of individuals.

> Hegel's liberal critics are in the habit of saying that he does not believe in founding a social order on the conception of individual rights. The element of truth in this assertion is that Hegel thinks personal right, apart from a developed system of ethical life, is an empty abstraction; he believes that a social order founded (as in liberal political theory) on such abstractions will be unable even to protect individual rights, much less to actualize the whole of concrete freedom. – Nisbet and Wood 1991: xvi

In contrast to liberalism and communitarianism, socialism takes equality to be the basic ideal and justifies coercive institutions insofar as they promote equality. In capitalist societies, the means of production are owned and controlled by a relatively small number of people and used basically for their benefit; socialists favour taking control of the means of production and redirecting their use to the general welfare. According to Marx, the principle of distribution for a socialist society is: from each according to ability, to each, according to needs. Socialists disagree among themselves. Then the question arises: who should control the means of production in a socialist society? The supporters of the socialism did not reach a unitary conclusion in this regard. In the version of socialism favoured by Lenin, those who control the means of production are to be an elite group, seemingly differing only in their ends from the capitalist elite they replaced. In other forms of socialism, the means of production are to be controlled democratically. In advanced capitalist societies, national defence, police and fire protection, income redistribution and environmental protection are already under democratic control. Democracy is thought to apply in these areas and to require some form of representation.

Human Rights

The concept of right arose in Roman jurisprudence and was extended to ethics via the theory of natural law (Audi 1999: 796). Just as positive law, the law posited by human lawmakers, confers legal rights, so the natural law confers natural rights. Rights are classified by their specific sources in different sorts of rules. Legal rights are advantageous positions under the law of a particular society. Again, different institutional rights are conferred by the rules of private organizations according to the moral code of a society. Some people identify natural law with moral law and often identify natural rights to our most fundamental rights and contrast them with ordinary moral rights. Recently, many politicians emphasize on human rights in describing the significance of rights. Some rights may be treated as human rights, viz. political, social, economical, etc. because these rights may be treated as necessary and legal rights. That is, human rights mean those rights which are essential and legal as a human being. So, independence, equality, environment, etc. are the living tools of a human being. "Vienna Declaration and Programme of Action" which was held in 1993 where human rights are described as universal, non-devisable and related concepts. Though human rights protect humans' natural rights, the universal Declaration of Human Rights, accepted by the United Nations Organization (UNO) in 1948, is the ultimate criterion. Besides this, some rights have included in later UNO conventions (Source: https: www.un.org/en/global-issues/human rights).

1. The punishment and damage against inhuman, cruel, undignified behaviour.
2. The legal system for the eradication of racial inequality.
3. Protection for the women from physical and mental harassment.
4. Protection for children.
5. Protection for the minority and the backward people.

Human rights play very much the same role in ethics once played by natural rights. Human rights are conceived more broadly to include positive social and economic rights, such as the right to social security or to an adequate standard of living.

Human rights refer to the concept of human beings as having universal rights, apart from legal jurisdiction. The concept of 'human rights' is based on religious principles. A formal concept of human rights has not been universally accepted (Talwar 2006: 1). Human rights are said to be those benefits to which we are entitled simply as human beings, thus the basis of the claim to rights should be something that differentiates humans from other animals.

So, human rights are literally the rights that one has simply as a human being. As such, they are equal rights, because we are all equal human beings, though, democracy and human rights both are different notions. When democracy aims at empowering the people collectively, human rights aim at empowering individuals. Democracy is interrelated with human rights to have equal and non-discriminating rights, especially for marginalized groups including women, minorities and children. Democracy is also linked to the protection of rights related to language, religion and ethnicity. These types of rights cannot be realized in a non-democratic system and likewise no democracy is sustainable without the presence of these rights.

Rights are also classified by status. Civil rights are those one possesses as a citizen, human rights are possessed by virtue of being a human. I assume that women's rights, children's rights, patients' rights, etc. are similar types.

Relation between Democracy and Human Rights

I have already mentioned that democracy and human rights both have different notions. While democracy aims at empowering the people collectively, human rights aim at empowering individuals. Democracy is also interrelated with human rights, especially for the marginalized groups. Democracy is also linked to the protection of rights related to language, religion and ethnicity. On the other hand, human rights are civil, political, economic, social and cultural. These types of rights cannot be realized in a non-democratic system and, likewise, no democracy is sustainable without the presence of these rights.

If we want to protect human rights, we have to ensure that people receive some degree of decent human treatment. Because, political systems that protect human rights are thought to reduce the threat of world conflict, all nations have a stake in promoting worldwide respect for human rights. International human rights law, humanitarian intervention law and refugee law all protect the right to life and physical integrity and attempt to limit the unrestrained power of the state. These laws aim to preserve humanity and protect against anything that challenges people's health, economic well-being, social stability and political peace. Underlying such laws consist of the principle of non-discrimination, the notion that rights apply universally. Consequently, the duty to protect human rights resides first and foremost with the states themselves. However, in many cases public authorities and government officials institute policies that violate basic human rights. Such abuses of power by political leaders and public authorities have devastating effects, including genocide, war crimes and crimes against humanity (Talwar 2006: 241).

Problem of Democracy

My observation in this respect is that we are not able to protect human rights until we get rid of the problem of democracy. We have seen that there are many internal as well as external problems in a particular state. The main problem is inequality, viz. social, cultural, economic, educational, language, etc. The actual democracy would not be possible if the people are unequal in different respects of a particular state. Consequently, the human rights cannot be a success until and unless the real democracy is established. In this paper, I want to show that if we make a situation of democracy proper, then human rights will be effective, otherwise not.

We can divide the democratic rule into two ways: one is pure or direct democracy and the other is indirect or representative democracy. Direct democracy means a particular rule of democracy where every citizen participates in the election. There was a time in Greece where people had participated in the rule directly. There people were involved in every activity, such as, formations of laws, implementation of laws, judgements, etc. There was no way to send representatives of the people. History teaches us that this direct democracy was introduced not only in Greece but also in Rome.

On the other hand, indirect or representative democracy is conducted by some representatives who are elected by the general public. In the present time, indirect democracy is prevailing in most countries, due to a large number of population and wide geographical spread. If we look at any state, it will be observed that the state has performed many activities which were not possible for the people directly. The indirect or representative democracy has two important features: one, rule of constitutional body is formed by some representatives who are elected by a general election and they have the responsibility or obligation to the people. And the second feature is to emphasize on political party.

There are some inconveniences or drawbacks of representative democracy, such as:

1. The representatives may be tyrants as they feel that the people are with them and people are supporting their decisions. They not only disregard their duties but also conduct government or government institution for their own whims and fancies. This type of government may detach itself from the ideal of welfare of the people and may create a barrier to the rights of people and their independence.
2. We have seen in many cases where representatives are not eligible in conducting government and they are inefficient in different ways. So, there is a possibility that the bureaucracy practises high handedness and thereby a bureaucratic rule may come into vogue. They may be usually indifferent to the problems of the common people. Illiterate and innocent

people cannot do anything distinctly and also rightly. Every time, the welfare of the majority is dominated by the welfare of the minority. Hamilton expresses his opinion about the tendency of the ruling authority in democracy in a clear and distinct way. He says: "Give all powers to many, they will oppress the few. Give all powers to few, they will oppress the many." (Anthony Scott et al. 2008: 48) We get same type of feeling from Aristotle's point of view. In politics, where he says that the constitution falls into three subdivisions on the basis of number, such as kingship, aristocracy and constitutional government (Barker 1998: 101). These three subdivisions have three wrong types, which are tyranny, oligarchy and democracy. Tyranny is the perversion of kingship, oligarchy is the perversion of aristocracy and democracy is the perversion of constitutional government. Tyranny is a government by a single person directed to the interest of that person, oligarchy is directed to the interest of well-to-do and democracy is directed to the interest of the poor. So, none of these constitutions is aware of the benefits of the common interest.

3. A representative government many times faces different types of malpractices which arise from class-rule government, such as, selfishness of the same class, struggle for authority, wastage of money, tendency to accept bribe or tendency to taking the illegal gratification, etc. These tendencies are opposed to real democracy.

How Can We Overcome These?

We have not overcome these types of problems in any democratic set-up in any country till now, but we have to admit that democratic rule is the ideal form of government, compared to other forms. It may create some problems in the establishment of democracy, because of its different methods and lack of proper implementation. But there is no reason to drop democracy and to underestimate its success. That is why most of the countries have accepted democracy as a political and social organization in the East as well as in the West.

Marxists put up many complaints against the general explanation of democracy. They argue that though democracy is the rule of every person, in practice, it actually invites the rule of some persons. According to them, democracy and inequality cannot run together. In a society where every way of production and material of production is totally acquired by some people and other people are totally deprived of this, democracy and liberty are useless. That is why Marxists always try to overcome or stop the uneven distribution of wealth and privilages in the society. They opine that a proper democracy is not possible until we are able to eliminate this inequality.

In this context, Marxist opinion is that the root of our social sufferings lies in our social system, and the social revolution led by the proletariat will bring us into a better world – to a social system, which will ultimately mature into a classless society. They thought that after the inevitable revolution a classless society is bound to come where the authority will lose its power. So, the fundamental problem of politics is to initiate the revolutionary activity (Bhattacharya 2012: 43-44).

Problem of Marxian Theory from Poppers Point of View

Karl Popper is one of those very few twentieth-century philosophers who have given us the solution to the problem of democracy. He tries to explain what the actual problem behind it is. He first felt a crisis in the essentialist commitment of the contemporary political ideology. Popper does not believe in the theory of revolution, because history teaches us that a revolution is liable to replace old matters by new ones. Who can guarantee that the new ones will be better? If it is true then what is the necessity to do another revolution? Popper holds:

> The theory of revolution overlooks the most important aspects of social life – that what we need are not so much good men as good institutions. Even the best man may be corrupted by the power; but institutions which permit the ruled to exert some effective control over the rulers will force even the bad rulers to do what the ruled consider to be in their interest. Or put it another way, we should like to have rulers, but experience shows us that we are not likely to get them. That is why it is of such importance to design institutions which prevent even bad rulers from causing too much damage.
>
> – Popper 1972: 344

Marxists, of course, thought in terms not of institutions but of classes. But classes, however, never rule any more than nation. The rulers are always certain persons. And whatever class they may once have belonged to, once they are rulers they belong to the ruling class, says Popper. Thus, the problem of controlling the rulers and of checking their power is, according to Popper, the main problem of politics. Popper accuses Marxists that they never realized the danger inherent in a policy of increasing the power of the state.

By democracy, Popper does not mean just the election of government by a majority of the governed, but the preservation of certain kinds of free institution which enable the ruled effectively to criticize their rulers and to change them without bloodshed.

Conclusion

My observation in this respect is that the solution to the problems for establishing real democracy, which is given by Karl Popper is fully correct. But if we want to have a practical shape of it, we have to give proper education to the people. Those people who are the blind supporters of any political party, they do not think that the political party to which they belong cannot do anything wrong. So, they cannot overcome the biasness, but if they get proper education then they may change their previous dogma. That is why, we have to take steps to create awareness among people, and consequently, we may reach the status of real democracy and fulfil our rights.

References

Anthony Scott, K., Thomas Jefferson and Alexander Hamilton, 2008, *A Defining Political Debate*, Boca Raton, Florida: Universal Publishers.

Audi, R., 1999, *The Cambridge Dictionary of Philosophy*, Cambridge: Cambridge University Press.

Barker, Ernest, 1998, *Aristotle Politics*, New York: Oxford University Press.

Bhattacharya, K., 2012, "Popper's Comprehensive Philosophical Worldview", *Jadavpur Journal of Philosophy*, 22.

Bryce, L.J., 1962, *Modern Democracies*, vol. 1, Calcutta: World Press.

Dicey, A.V. Kings Counsel, 1905, *Law and Public Opinion in England*, London: Macmillan & Co.

Green T.H., 1999, *Lectures on the Principles of Political Obligation*, Kitchener, Ontario: Batoche Books.

Laslett, Peter and John Locke, 1960, *Two Treatises of Government*, Cambridge: Cambridge University Press.

Lincoln's Gettysburg Address, 1863, delivered on November 19. (Source: https://www.loc.gov/item/today-in-history/november-19/)

Nisbet, H.B. (tr.), and Allen W. Wood (ed.), 1991, *G.W.F. Hegel, Elements of the Philosophy of Right*, Cambridge: Cambridge University Press.

Popper, K., 1972, *Conjectures and Refutations*, London: Routledge & Kegan Paul.

Talwar, P., 2006, *Human Rights*, Delhi: Isha Books.

Yalf, David A. and Kenneth Dautrich, 2011, *American Government: Historical, Popular, and Global Perspectives*, Boston: Wadsworth Publishing Co.

5

Norms of Democracy in Buddhist Thought
Ideas and Implementation

Gouri Sankar Bandyopadhyay

Introduction

> Religion of the Buddha gives freedom of thought and freedom of self-development to all. The rise of Buddhism in India was as significant as the French Revolution. – B.R. Ambedkar

THE present study attempts humbly to articulate the historical role of Gautama Buddha and his noble ideas in the formation of basic norms of democracy. Plethora of literary evidences preserved in the vast Buddhist literature especially Pāli literature portray Gautama Buddha as a progressive socio-religious reformer as well as an unparallel and prudent political thinker. One of the prime objectives of the study is to focus on Buddhist views and thoughts related to the spread of democratic ideas in early India highlighting Saṅgha, the classless and casteless monastic organization. Scholars like Rhys Davids presented the Buddha as a great personality who made the clarion call of human liberty and conceded equality among all human beings, a cardinal principle in a democratic society (1899, vol. 1: 96). In his own voice the Buddha said:

> Take ye refuge unto yourself; be ye your own salvation. With earnestness and high resolve work out your own salvation.

He vividly pointed out the absolute folly of artificial distinctions between man and man. At his own time, there was a rigid caste system in India. The Buddha, in fact, revolted against this unjust and asserted the principles of equality of all men as far as their fundamental rights are concerned. Ambedkar branded Buddhism as upholding the democratic principles both in religion as well as in society. Indeed, he found variants of humanism in the Indian civilization through the lense of Buddhism. He rejected Hinduism because he believed that the caste system was co-substantial to this religion, whereas equality was inherent in Buddhism (Jaffrelot and Narender 2018). Ambedkar loudly declared:

> My philosophy has roots in religion and not in political science. I have derived them from the teachings of my Master, the Buddha. In his philosophy, liberty and equality had a place. He gave the highest place to fraternity as the only real safeguard against the denial of liberty or equality or fraternity which was another name for brotherhood or humanity; this was again another name for religion. – Ibid.: 503

A large section of scholars holds the view that the cognitive aspect of early Buddhist philosophy was far less important than the ethical. The Buddha himself did not pay much attention to purely metaphysical questions, believing that what was most important was to preach the right path in life. His teachings were mostly ornamented by early Indian materialism. He and his followers accepted that

> *Dharma* can be those of the senses, related to perception of the material world (whatever can be seen, heard, etc.), *dharma* of consciousness (abstract notions) and several other categories, including things not subject to existence and striving for peace – *nirvāṇa*. – Tokarev 1989: 308-09

The Buddha stood against exploitation, and social and economic inequality, injustices and his sincere appeal attracted especially the poor, downtrodden and marginalized population (Kosambi 1956: 162). He was determined to establish and preserve democratic environment inside his Saṅgha as well as in the greater human society. These unique characteristics endorsed with democratic spirit once made Buddhism invincible in India and beyond its boundary. The Buddha's teachings met both the mundane and spiritual needs together and desires of various sections of population. He did not deny explicitly the existence of gods, and simultaneously he taught that the gods could not liberate man from the misery of existence (Tokarev 1989: 310). Indeed, it is generally believed that when early Indian Brāhmanical political thought propagated for kingship and monarchical form of government, the Buddhist political thought stood for democracy and republican form of government.

The Buddha, "Saṅgha" and Democracy

Scholars and political thinkers considered Buddhism as a democratic religion, and particularly Ambedkar, eventually found in this religion the societal values and tried to promote it via political democracy. In time of preaching his religion the Buddha being a reformer never gave emphasis on the pride of the birth, pedigree and lineage. In this respect, Buddhism is identical with European Protestantism or Lutheranism. The Buddha used to give importance to wisdom, good actions and righteousness:

> There is no reference to the question either of birth, or of lineage or of the pride which says: "you are held as worthy, as I" or "you are not held as worthy as I". It is only by having got rid of all such bondage that one can realize for himself that supreme perfection in wisdom and in conduct. – Rhys Davids 1899: 123

He always did keep his faith on democratic ideas and principles denying casteism and socio-economic status within his monastic order. Chattopadhyay (1992: 460-61) succinctly observes:

> Within the Buddhist order there could have been no distinction between the higher and the lower castes, or even between the king and the slave. Buddha once asked king Ajātaśatru that if a slave of the royal household left the palace; took to the yellow robe of the Order and lived the life of a monk without reproach in thought, word or deed, would you then say, let the man come back and be a slave again? And the king answered: "Nay, Lord, rather should we greet him with reverence, and rise up from our seat out of deference towards him, and press him to be seated."
>
> – *Dialogues of the Buddha*, vol. 1, p. 77

Undoubtedly, the Buddha's religion was principally related to the well-being of the people of all categories irrespective of regions, and he addressed himself "to the welfare of many people, to the joy of many people, to the blessing, welfare and joy of gods and men" (*bahujanahitāya, bahujanasukhāya*) (Oldenberg 1927: 157). Few examples, revealing the Buddha's crusade against caste–class discrimination should be mentioned here. The most influential and powerful disciple of Gautama Buddha and the most distinguished member of his Order was Upāli, who was formerly a barber (Rhys Davids 1899: 102). Again, Sunitā, one of the brethren whose verses are selected for inclusion in the esteemed *Theragāthā*, was a "Pukkusa", one of the low tribes of early India (ibid.). All these reflect an unbiased and egalitarian attitude of both Tathāgata Buddha and his unique monastic order – Saṅgha. One of the Buddhist innovations was opening the membership of the Order to all castes, *varṇas*, genders and classes. A section of critics argues that Buddhism, especially in its formative days, was patronized and encouraged by the monarchs, merchants and aristocrats, and it helped the expansion of the mighty Magadhan Empire as well as the Magadhan trade to some extent. But in true sense,

> the Buddha was acting only as an unconscious tool of history, and Buddhism, from its very inception, was destined to become perhaps the biggest socio-religious movement in Indian history.
>
> – Chattopadhyay 1992: 466

There is hardly any doubt that the Buddha's attitude to the injustices of caste system or to the barrenness of the Brāhmanical socio-religious rites and rituals might have been significant factors accounting for its appeal to the people of all sections. Ambedkar realized the truth that this rediscovery of Buddhism had important implications. If teaching of the Buddha was democratic, then democracy is not an invention of the West. In his belief it is a product of the Indian history. In his historic speech of 25 November 1949 where Ambedkar presented the final draft of the Indian Constitution to the Assembly which was to pass it on 26 January 1950, he emphatically pointed out that by becoming a parliamentary constituency "again", India is back to its Buddhist roots. It is not that India did not know parliamentary procedure. A study of the Buddhist Bhikṣu Saṅghas discloses that not only there were parliaments — for the Saṅghas were nothing but parliaments — but the Saṅghas knew and observed all the rules of parliamentary procedure known to modern times.

In the formation of Saṅgha, the Buddha incorporated deliberately the democratic principles and practices in optimum level. He asked the people to join his Saṅghas, and the Saṅghas were modelled mostly on the pattern of the early Indian tribal democracies or republics. Moreover, the Buddha gave equal status to women and opened the door of his Saṅgha for them, and thus rejected gender discrimination emphatically at the dawn of human civilization. The *Dīgha Nikāya*, the *Majjhima Nikāya* and the *Saṁyutta Nikāya* and other early Buddhist Pāli texts mention many courtesans (*janapada kalyāṇī*) who fed the Buddha and his disciples and presented gifts to the Order. He properly understood that without active participation of the women irrespective of caste, colour and class, democracy within Saṅgha never be restored or protected. The Buddha unhesitatingly admitted to his Order of Monks also people of the so-called low castes — barbers, butchers, sweepers and the untouchable along with the members of the noble and priestly castes. He announced:

No man is noble by birth,
No man is ignoble by birth.
Man is noble by his own deeds,
Man is ignoble by his own deeds.

Khongchinda observes in this context that the style of functioning of the Buddhist is democratic, both in form and spirit. This form can be said to have been designed by the Buddha. It will not be too fanciful to say that the Buddha was the first to have thought of and to have formed a democratic government (Kongchinda 2015). He states further:

> The minority of the Saṅgha is also respected. All *bhikkhus* in the assembly or in the monastery have equal right to do all Saṅgha affairs. – Ibid.

The word "democracy" is derived from the Greek words *demos* (the people) and *kratos* (power or rule), and such democracy is the government of the, by the, and for the people. Dhammarama comments explicitly that there is an affinity between Buddhism and democracy. The Buddha appeared on account of democracy at a time when autocracy was prevalent in India (Dhammarama 2016). It is also argued:

> Even though Buddhist principles and democracy have very close relationship, the doctrine preached by the Buddha is not based on political philosophy. Sometimes the Buddha is said to be a social reformer and he condemned the caste system, recognized the equality of people. – Ibid.

For its very existence and expansion, Buddhism had to fight against powerful caste-based Brāhmanical socio-economic-political system. Especially, economy in true sense played an extremely pivotal role in Buddhist Order. A.N. Bose brilliantly observed:

> As in Europe of the eighteenth century it is seen that the economic content of democratic movements was the struggle of the rising bourgeoisie to seize power from the grip of the firmly entrenched

> clergy and nobles, so the ideal of Buddhist republicanism was the replacement of the brāhmaṇa priesthood by the *seṭṭhis* and *gahapatis* and their royal allies. Against the Brāhmanical pretention to supremacy explicit in the fourfold caste order ... the Buddhist works give precedence to khatriyas over the brāhmaṇa, *gahapati* and *sudda* and often burst into vigorous denunciation of the brāhmaṇa with their sacrificial rites and sordid motives of gain. – 1945: 481-82

It was told in the *Ambaṭṭhasutta*, a reputed Pāli literature (ibid.) that "The khatriyas are superior, the brāhmaṇas are inferior". In other words,

> the mercantile interest served the Saṅgha as lay *upāsakas*, built there *caityas* and *stūpas*, fed them with choice delicacies and rose to power and position. – Ibid.: 482

However, one of the important precepts of Buddhism is love and charity to all living beings in the world.

Shadow of the Early Indian Republican Heritage in Buddhist Political Thought

The *saṅgha* means Buddhist monastic community and the early Buddhist communities (Saṅghas) were nothing but brotherhoods of impoverished monks (*bhikṣus*) and female celibates (*bhikṣuṇīs*). From the Buddha's time they could be joined by people from different castes, with the exception of slaves, soldiers, criminals, debtors and individuals whose parents were opposed. The rules of the Saṅghas were strict; no one could have any property except for simple clothing that was yellow (yellow was considered the colour of the poor, "impure" castes), they lived on charity, ate once a day before the sunset, and took vows of charity (Tokarev 1989: 310). It was recognized that

> the Saṅgha was largely a self-regulatory social institution, a semi-autonomous association that was bound to witness competing interpretive understandings of what consisted the true teachings

> and practices leading to the final religious goal. Because of these competing understandings regarding details of the *dharma* and *vinaya* of the Buddha, a series of monastic councils were convened in the centuries following the Buddha's demise to settle the inevitable disputes that had arisen. – Padma and Holt 1998: 4

The Buddha himself, though a friend of kings or monarchs, seems to have had a deep affection for the old republican organization, and in a remarkable passage he is said to have warned the Vr̥jjis shortly before his death that their security depended on maintaining their traditions and holding regular and well-attended folk-moots (Norbu 2020). It is properly argued that the then existing and simultaneously decaying tribal republican communities of northern and eastern India popularly known as *gaṇa*s inspired Gautama Buddha to form his Saṅgha, the monastic organization, based on the ideas of democracy. Years ago, Jayswal (1924: 45-55) mentioned that the Buddha was consciously looking at the *gaṇa*s or Saṅghas, prevailed in the sixth century BCE as model of his own monastic order. He took the Saṅghas to be ancient republican states. Majumdar (1919: 286-328) also expressed almost similar views. Chattopadhyay further argues:

> The Buddha never forgot the pride of belonging to the Śākya tribe. One of the most typical forms in which the texts referred to him was "Son of the Śākyas" (Śākyaputta) and later "Śākya Muni"). He was full of reverence for the ancestral (republican) institutions; the tribal institutions – a prominent feature of which the Buddha was himself so proud of, was, during his own lifetime, threatened by the emergent state-powers. – 1992: 472-73

Evidently, the Buddha had witnessed the destruction of the tribal republics and autonomous principalities (*gaṇa*s or Saṅghas) by the hands of imperialist state-powers like Magadha in his times. Ajātaśatru's invasion on the confederacy of the Vajjians was invariably a part of the policy of the rising imperial powers to destruct the Saṅghas. The Vedic-Brāhmanical political thought, compiled later in the Kauṭilya's *Arthaśāstra* prescribes:

> There was no prospect of the rising monarchs so long as the free Saṅghas – too strong to be destroyed by direct military action – survived in the neighbourhood. Besides, the example of their democracy was considered dangerous for the monarchs.
>
> – 1992: 473

Even the Buddha could not stop the disaster of his own tribe – "Sākyas". He had to witness the massacre of his own people by the mightiest imperial power of his age. The emergence of the Magadhan state especially followed the same pattern of violent extermination of the tribal democracies. He saw his own people, including women and children, being ruthlessly thrashed and exterminated. It is noted that the Buddha's ideal kingdom was based on truth, peace and collective righteousness. He says:

> I have gained coolness and have obtained *nirvāṇa*. To find the kingdom of truth I went to city of Kāśīs. ...– SBE, XIII: 91

It is argued that the lost collective life ever lingered in the Buddhist tradition and was looked upon as the golden age of the past. And consequently, the Buddha was modelling consciously his Order – Saṅgha – on the surviving tribal democracies. It is stated in the *Dīgha Nikāya*:

> The memory of a classless, undifferentiated society remained as the legend of a golden age when the good earth spontaneously produced ample food without labour, men had neither property nor greed. – Chattopadhyay 1992: 162

Similar view has been reflected in the *Mahāvastu Avadāna*, one of the old resourceful Buddhist texts:

> In the beginning people used to feed on love and live in the abodes which was bliss. And whatever they did was *dhamma*. Then emerged among them the distinction of *varṇa* (colour); some had good *varṇa*, some bad. Vanity was thus born and with its birth died *dhamma*. And with it dried up love and honey on which they were so long feeding. Thereafter the idea of hoarding the grain gradually grew in their minds. And the greed for hoarding

> went on increasing. Along with it dawned the consciousness of the difference between the sexes. Once everybody assembled together and resolved: "Come, let us elect somebody from amongst ourselves to look after the border of each one's field. He will be strong and intelligent and fair to all. ..." Thus, they elected one among themselves. On the consent of all, he became a *rājā*. That is why the *rājā* is called a *mahā-sāmanta*, the Great Consent.
>
> – Shastri 2011: 142

One can find easily its deep resemblance with the basic ideas of Rousseau (*The Social Contract*) and of Friedrich Engels (*The Origin of the Family, Private Property and the State*).

The above legends revealing the archaic spirits of tribal democracies are almost unparallel in early Indian literature outside Buddhism. Chattopadhyay opines justifiably:

> In any case, passages like these show that the memory of the lost collective life was never completely wasted away from the Buddhist tradition and that such a life was looked upon as the golden age of the past. It was such a life, again, which the Buddha had in mind when he spoke of the kingdom of Truth or Righteousness.
>
> – 2011: 485

From such viewpoint, the Saṅgha in Buddhist tradition promoted mostly the democratic principles and practices for a better world in future. His Holiness the 14th Dalai Lama once stated properly assessing the role of the Buddha in the formation of Saṅgha, based on sheer democratic concepts:

> The institution the Buddha established was the Saṅgha or monastic community, which functioned on largely democratic lines. Within this fraternity, individuals were equal, whatever their social class or caste origins. ... Within the community decisions were taken by vote and difference were by consensus. Thus, the Saṅgha served as a model for social equality, sharing of resources and democratic process.[1]

---

[1] His Holiness the 14th Dalai Lama, in his speech titled "Buddhism and Democracy", Washington DC, April 1993.

The Buddha's Concept of Democracy: The Emergence of Early Indian Materialism

Years ago, H.C. Warren brilliantly assessed the unique character of the Buddhist Saṅghas. Unlike Christ, the Buddha instituted an Order, or Church, during his own lifetime; and in the course of his long ministry of forty-five years, and as occasion arose, he made a great many regulations for its guidance (Warren 1898: 392). Most important factors behind the success of early Buddhism were monastic discipline (*vinaya*) and autonomous-cum-egalitarian ideas and policies. It is stated that the conception of society in the political philosophy of ancient India was that of an aggregate composed of units of diverse kinds – learned bodies, village communities, religious corporations, etc. Each was regarded as subject to its own system of law, called *sāmya* (conventional law) in ancient Indian jurisprudence. Among these societal units, the Buddhist Saṅgha became one, an "association group" functioning under a system of law of its own (Dutt 1962: 80-81). For the Saṅgha, this *sāmya* was *vinaya*. Early *vinaya* ritual traditions consisting of *prātimokṣa* and *pavaraṇa* (collective rites of Saṅgha to monastic code of disciplines) created a binding moral effect upon the community that also sustained an ethos of egalitarian collectivity and responsibility (Padma and Holt 1998: 3).

The underlying truth behind the entire endeavour was that the Buddha had been radically departed from the other organizers of religious or monastic groups during or before his times in making the surviving free tribes of his times the models for Saṅghas, founded by him. Chattopadhyay further argues:

> The Saṅghas were consciously designed by him to be illusory substitutes for what was being systematically annihilated in reality.
>
> – 1992: 483

The "Mahāparinibbānasutta", a part of the *Dīgha Nikāya*, one of the highly popular Pāli scriptures, records an interesting legend which symbolizes the Buddha's attitude against imperialistic expansion, responsible for the annihilation of the democratic forces. Once, Magadhan king Ajātaśatru in time of his offensive against the Vajjians sent his minister, the brāhmaṇa Vassakara to the Buddha seeking his blessings adding:

> Whatever the Blessed One should answer you, keep it well in mind and inform me; for Tathāgata [one who are thus gone] do not speak falsely.

The Buddha avoiding Vassakara told to his disciple and cousin Ananda:

> So long, Ananda, as the Vajjians forgather thus often, and frequent the public meetings of their clan; so long may they be expected not to decline but to prosper.[2]

And the Magadhan minister, failing to obtain the Buddha's blessings, left the place. In another account, the Buddha presents to Vassakara "seven principles for a nation's welfare". At the end of the discourse, the minister concludes:

> No harm, indeed, can be done to the Vr̥jjis in battle by Magadha's king, Ajātaśatru, except through treachery or discord.

In fact, the Buddha had full respects to the *gaṇas* and Saṅghas, the democratic peoples' assemblies. In either telling, the Buddha lays out seven qualities that lead to a republic's prosperity. The Buddha's questions are thus a litmus test for the health of a nation and are worth asking again today (Norbu 2020).

Consequently, one may argue that it was indeed not an accident that the Buddha adopted the name "Saṅgha" meaning the tribal democratic society, for his own Order. Jayswal reminds us that

> the Buddha was born in a republican people. He had Saṅgha neighbours around him, and he grew up amongst them. He called the community which he founded *bhikkhu* Saṅgha, or the republican of the *bhikkus*. He, probably following his

[2] Mahaparinibbanasutta, iii.

> contemporary teachers, adopted the name as well as the constitution of the political Saṅgha in founding his religious Saṅgha.
> – 1924: 45

The Buddhist Saṅghas were democratic and to some extent socialistic in nature. Majumdar opines:

> The general assembly of the monks constituted the sovereign authority and the procedure of its meetings was laid down with minute exactness. ... No meeting was legal unless all the members entitled to vote were either present, or being absent, formally declared their consent.
> – 1919: 310-11

The distinguished Buddhist text *Mahāvagga* II.18 mentions a lot of rules regarding voting procedure and system of quorum of the Buddhist Saṅghas. According to Chattopadhyay, such an ultra-democratic constitution was not an innovation of the Buddha; it was simply brilliant imitation of the earlier tribal democracies (1992: 489). The *Mahāvagga* II.18 also mentions categorically the casting of votes by the *bhikkhus* of the Saṅghas using voting tokens (*salākā*/or *daṇḍasalākā*). In a similar way, the *Vinaya Piṭaka* reveals the Buddha's deep concern for inner-Saṅgha democracy:

> ... If an official act, Oh *bhikkhus*! is performed unlawfully by an incompetent congregation, it is no real act and ought not to be performed, etc. If an official act, Oh *bhikkhus*! is performed against which (the *bhikkhus* present) protest, which is unlawful, objectionable, and invalid, this is no real act and ought not to be performed. ...
> – XVII: 256-58

German scholar Egon Flaig also discussed elaborately about the democratic spirits found in early Pāli texts — the Pāli Vinaya, especially the *Mahāparinibbānasuttanta*, the *Mahāvagga* and the *Cullavagga* which became part of the canon by fourth and third century BCE. He explained that all these texts reveal that in the Buddhist Order majority voting emerged as perhaps the central way in which decisions should be made within the monastic community. Voting was held by secret ballot (using voting sticks) or by show of hands, or by whispering one's preference into another monk's ear. At the same time, if there was a dispute about how monastic rules are to be applied, the decision could be taken by a committee elected for the purpose as well as by a majority vote in the monastic assembly (Flaig 2013; Kierstead 2018). Besides, the Saṅghas knew and observed all the rules of parliamentary procedure known to modern times. They had rules regarding seating arrangements, motions, resolutions, quorum, whip, censure motion, regularization and so on. Flaig tried to come into conclusion that the Buddhist monasteries were more democratic than the Indian city states (Flaig 2013). But on the other hand, the earliest Buddhists received some democratic ideas from the republican city states of ancient India (Kierstead 2018). In other words, the Buddha must have borrowed these rules of parliamentary procedure from the political assemblies functioning in the country in his times.

Regarding private or individual ownership of property, early tribal societies followed the socialistic principles with eternal nature. Within the Saṅghas the Buddha made effort to impose those communistic principles of private relations. Majumdar explained it in such way,

> the individual in the Buddhist Church was merged in the corporation. The same relation between the individual and the corporation is brought out by the general presumption in the Buddhist Canon Law that everyday belongs to the Saṅgha and not to any individual monk, and that the latter can only possess that which has been sufficiently allotted to him. ... Even when things were allowed to a *bhikkhu* for his personal use, they were considered as the property of the Saṅgha. It is perfectly in keeping with this doctrine that on the death of a *bhikkhu*, the Saṅgha became the owner of his property. – 1919: 316-18

The Buddhist scriptures in Pāli (SBE III.18n; Chattopadhyay 1992: 493) stated it clearly that

> at the end of the *vassa* period (rainy season) the Saṅgha, or community of brothers in any place, was accustomed to give over

> to someone of the *bhikkhus* such store of robes as it possessed; and it should here be observed that no *bhikkhu* had a separate personal ownership over his robes, though normally given to him for his own use, and really his own subject to the rules, they were technically speaking, the property of the whole Saṅgha.

The above evidences strongly unearth the fact that the Buddha felt firmly against private property and individual possession within the Order. He believed scientifically like a sizeable group of our modern sociologists and political philosophers-scientists that the private property was the root cause of all sorts of greed and corruptions. The natural corollary is that the Buddha had not such enough power to reform the whole society, but within his order – the ideal Saṅgha – his power and determination were supreme, unchallenged. He could not permit it to be dictated by the power of gold (Chattopadhyay 1992: 493). In the Saṅgha, there was a reference to *pacittya* offence involving forfeiture (CBSE XIII.26). Emphasizing the inherent democratic values and principles of the Saṅgha in comparison with our present concepts of democracy Spellmeyer (2017) observes:

> But what about the Saṅgha the Buddha organized? When we search our planet for democracies today, we look to institutions of governments that remind us of our own. We like to see free and fair elections that include all or most adults. We expect to find arrangements similar to Britain's parliament or our Congress. Our picture of democracy gets rounded out with a codified body of laws and independent judiciary. By this standard, the early Saṅgha does look democratic. Any gathering of monks operated like Greek assembly. The Saṅgha even had the *vinaya*, a legal code of sorts.

Again, the Buddha condemned slavery in any shape and form. He laid down golden rules for the right manner of earning one's living in a way not harmful to others, and this included also that any trafficking in human beings was out of bounds for a Buddhist (Kirthisinghe 2011). He also preached the gospel of tolerance, of compassion, loving kindness and non-violence. Following the basic norms of a democratic society he taught men not to despise other religions and not to belittle them.

Epilogue

At the end of this discourse after thorough review of the Buddhist Pāli literature, the following hypothesis can be drawn. The Buddhist materialism, reflected in origin and functioning of the Saṅgha organization with all its comprehensive ideas and practices made a great impression in social, cultural and political life of early India. The doctrine of *dhamma* constituted the very foundation of the Buddhist philosophy. It contains, although in naive and mystical form, the clear elements of dialectics (Tokarev 1989: 309). The dogma of early Buddhism is sometimes rightly called "religion without God", "atheist religion". One of the main factors responsible for wider popularity of Buddhism was its universal appeal to all sections of population. It is rightly stated that for urban classes, the khatriyas and other so-called low castes, Buddhism became a powerful weapon of struggle to fight against Brāhmanical supremacy and its unjust privileges, and against caste discrimination and class exploitation. For the oppressed masses and people from lower *varṇas*, who saw no way out of their poverty and distress, Buddhist teachings offered a radical alternative (ibid.: 310). Moreover, Buddhism in origin was gender neutral and this faith welcomed womenfolk to the Saṅghas. In short, the Saṅghas acted as an operative in this whole process of transformation from sixth century BCE. The Buddha looked upon the sufferings of his own age as a sickness, a disease and he projected his Saṅghas as the remedy for the removal of illness.

The Buddha in his famous Sermon at Benares stated clearly that it was the thirst and lust which lay behind the origin of suffering:

> This, Oh monks! is the sacred truth of the origin of suffering: it is the thirst (for being), which leads from birth to birth, together with lust and desire, which finds gratification here and there:

> the thirst of pleasure, the thirst for being, the thirst for power ... the extinction of this thirst by complete annihilation of desire, letting it go, expelling it, separating oneself from it, giving it no room. ... – Chattopadhyay 1992: 503

Gautama Buddha did not suggest self-annihilation or any kind of ascetic self-mortification to save the human society. Instead, he suggested the revival of the simple morality of the gentile society. So he asked the people to take the *pabajja* and the *upasampada* ordinations, i.e. "to go out" of the actual society and "to arrive at" the life of the Saṅghas. Indeed,

> the Saṅghas, as a classless society within the bosom of the class society, were but ideal substitutes for the vanished realities. – Yang 2016

There is then good evidence that democracy was something that Buddhists have long thought about and practised. The proposed study, based on early Indian Pāli literature has been successful to reveal that at a juncture of history when there was darkness and disappointment, the Buddha founded his Saṅghas, the classless democratic colonies for the mankind and these Saṅghas played the role of lighthouse for the well-being of the entire mankind. Indeed, there is hardly any question of the relevance of Saṅgha-induced democratic and socialistic ideas to our modern world. Yang holds the view:

> Democratic principles, collective leadership, and community empowerments are vital for continuing the *dharma* in the West — they are key elements in making these ancient teachings relevant for our complex contemporary world. – Leidecker 1963

Indeed, it is one of the basic assumptions of a democratic society that it is made up, and should be made up, of a variety of individuals whose individuality is guaranteed. This is also the meaning and intent of Buddhism. At the end of this discourse we may conclude that the Buddha devoted himself to build up a model society placing his Saṅghas in centre which would be free from caste consciousness, exploitation, gender disparity, moral deterioration and undemocratic practices.

References

Bose, A.N., 1945, *Social and Rural Economy of Northern India c.*600 BC 200 AD, vol. II, Calcutta: Firma K.L. Mukhopadhyay.

Chattopadhyay, D.P., 1992, *Lokayata: A Study of Ancient India Materialism*, 7th edn, New Delhi: People's Publishing.

Dhammarama, B., 2016, "Buddhist Principles on Democracy", *Education*, Colombo: Sri Lanka.

Dutt, Sukumar, 1962, *Buddhist Monks and Monasteries in India*, London: Allen and Unwin.

Flaig, Egon, 2013, *Die Mehrheitsentscheidung*, Berlin: De Gruyter.

His Holiness the 14th Dalai Lama, in his speech titled "Buddhism and Democracy", Washington DC, April 1993.

Jaffrelot, Christophe and Narender Kumar (eds), 2018, *Dr Ambedkar and Democracy: An Anthology*, New Delhi: Oxford University Press.

Jayswal, K.P., 1924, *Hindu Polity: A Constitutional History of India in Hindu Times*, 1st edn, Calcutta: Butterworth and Co.

Khongchinda, Phramatachanya, 2015 (Publishers), "The Third Stage of Development of Buddhist Sangha (Democracy)", *Buddhist Anarchism*, available at https://www.buddhapanaya.org/buddhaDocs., accessed in January.

Kierstead, James, 2018, "Democratic from the Start", in *Magazine Feature Society & Environment*, Spring (source: https: tricycle.org/magazine/buddhism-democratic-from-the-start).

Kirthisinghe, Buddhadasa P., 2011, "The Buddha and Democratic Principles", in *Buddhism and Democracy*, Kandy, Sri Lanka: Buddhist Publication Society.

Kosambi, D.D., 1956, *An Introduction to the Study of Indian History*, Bombay: Popular Book Depot.

Leidecker, K.F., 1963, "Buddhism in Democratic World", *Buddhism and Democracy*, Kandy, Sri Lanka: Buddhist Publication Society.

Majumdar, R.C., 1919, *Corporate Life in Ancient India*, Poona: The Oriental Book Agency.

Norbu, Jamyang, 2020, "The Buddha's Discourse on Defending Democracy", *Tricycle.*

Oldenberg, H., 1927, *Buddha: His Life, His Doctrines, His Order*, London: Williams and Norgate.

Padma, B. Sree and John Clifford Holt 1998, "Buddhism in Andhra and Its Influence on Buddhism in Sri Lanka", *The Indian Historical Review*, XXIII.

Rhys-Davids, T.W.R., 1899, *Dialogues of the Buddha*, vol. 1, London: Oxford University Press.

Shastri, H.P., 2011, *Bauddha Dharma* (in Bengali), Dhaka: Nabajuga Prokashani.

Spellmeyer, Kurt, 2017, "Is the Dharma Democratic?", *Tricycle* (Spring), available at https:// tricycle.org/topic/history-philosophy.

Tokarev, Sergei, 1989, *History of Religion*, Moscow: Progress Publishers.

Warren, H.C., 1898, *Buddhism in Translations* (HOS3), Cambridge, MA: Harward University Press.

Yang, Larry, 2016, "Democracy Is Good for Sanghas", *Lion's Roar*, 8 August. (source: https: www.lionroar.com/democracy-is-good-for-sanghas)

6

Quest for the Responsibilities to Make an Ideal Democratic State

Rajkumar Modak

> Our great democracies still tend to think that a stupid man is more likely to be honest than a clever man and our politicians take advantage of this prejudice by pretending to be even more stupid than nature made them. – Bertrand Russell

Introduction

CREATION of new ideas, new ways and new values and so on, for the need of the time, in order to increase the power of adaptability with the nature makes *Homo sapiens* not only different from the other sapiens such as *Homo neanderthalensis*, *Homo erectus*, *Homo soloensis*, *Homo floresiensis*, *Homo denisova*, *Homo rudolfensis* and *Homo ergaster* but also paves the way to exist in this planet as the superior to all other species. Other species, such as bees or ants or mosquitoes, have the tremendous power of adaptability, but the tremendous power, which they have got inherently, seems to be limited. It is limited, in this sense that they accept the nature, as they have been given, but on the other hand, human being, through his/her creative powers not only changes the nature, but also invents some unique principles which are self-imposed, at the same time, help him or her to reign in this earth for a long time. Among these self-created as well as self-imposed principles, democracy is mostly significant. It is significant from two respects: first, it is not just a fictitious idea, because it has the practical applicability, and second, it is one of the ideal systems of human being which needs to be sharpened again and again for the need of time, in order to be more effective.

In the *Cambridge Dictionary*, the term democracy has been defined as "the belief in freedom and equality between people, or a system of government based on this belief, in which the power is either held by the elected representatives or by the people themselves". From this definition, it is clear that democracy signifies a kind of authority which acts as that the kinetic power of a state through which a state can be the role model for the rest of the world, based on the belief in freedom as well as equality of the people. Again, this kinetic power is to be handed over to those persons who must be elected through a fair and justified process of election, so that the will of the common general people can be reflected following their belief in freedom and equality. Actually, in democracy, there must be a close relationship between "I" and "you". Though elected government authorities are supposed to be called by the term "you", from the perspective of the common general people, it will be one of the necessary conditions for the application of democracy in its optimum level, if the people realize that they are actually governed by themselves, i.e. to say there will be no insurmountable gap between "I" and "you". In the words of Abraham Lincoln, "Democracy is a government of the people, by the people, and for the people". But, one may argue against this definition that a kind of popularism seems to be favoured and the democracy may be failed to reach its destination. The justification of this objection seems to be legitimate, but it is somehow a different type of issue. However, one more point should be addressed here which is concerned with the notion of freedom. As it is a necessary condition for democracy, the concept of freedom and the boundary of freedom are to be discussed in detail; otherwise, democracy will be failed. Furthermore, the term equality which is used in the definition of the democracy is essential but at the same time it seems to be the most critical, though Aristotle defines a human being as a rational animal. An example will help to get the point, i.e. how critical the term equality is. In a hospital, suppose, ten children born at the same time; but each of them is different from one another, even the twins are also different. Again, the power of merit can never be the same. So, what type of equality has been sought for, in order to get success in democracy, is also one of the major points.

From the background mentioned above, the aim of this paper is to quest for the responsibilities how to make an ideal democratic state. Here, the term responsibility is very important, as it is the keyword of this paper. Following the proverb, "example is better than the definition" in order to get the meaning of the term; we are sure that being a human, we are bound to pay some responsibilities in our family life, social life as well as political life. From the perspective of our political life, social life as well as family life, as these three are mutually inclusive, the responsibilities and duties towards the ideal democratic state can be resumed.

Whose responsibilities will be the subject matter of this enquiry to make an ideal democratic state is clear, but the point is: what are the domains of the responsibilities? From the analysis of the definition of the democratic state, it is clear that we have to show our responsibilities mainly from the perspective of:

i. authority (who becomes the authority after the election),
ii. a fare election process,
iii. freedom, and
iv. equality.

Before delving upon the responsibilities of the said domains in order to establish a strong democracy, let us revisit some other definitions of democracy in detail, as made by the different thinkers, from the different perspectives, following the need of the time, otherwise this paper will be confined only to the said four domains of responsibilities. Be noted that the methodology of this paper is descriptive-cum-analytical. In fact, if the domains of responsibilities are clear to us, it will not only be helpful to justify our present position, but also useful to minimize the gap between the ideal and actual democracy.

The Definitions of Democracy

DEFINITION 1 [FROM CONSTITUTIONAL PERSPECTIVE]

At the time of Aristotle, the term democracy was not loaded with the same gravity of connotation, as it is now, though at that time, Greece was one of the developed countries of the world in all respects. Naturally, most of the citizens of Greece, at that time, were very much conscious about their right, culture, education and so on. From this perspective Aristotle defined democracy as:

> A constitution [or *politeia*] may be defined as the organization of a city or polis in respect of its offices generally, but especially in respect of that particular office which is sovereign in all issues. ... In democratic cities, for example, the people demosis sovereign. ... When the masses govern the city with a view to the common interest, the form of government is called by the generic name ... of "constitutional government". ... Democracy is directed to the interest of the poor only, not to the interests of everyone.
>
> – Aristotle 1995: 97-101

DEFINITION 2 [FROM THE PERSPECTIVE OF POWER]

Democracy is, in fact, a system through which a state is governed. Naturally, there are some persons who will be the administrators and liable to take any decision through the implementation of power. In monarchy, it was told that the words of the king were the rules, i.e. the king was the sole authority to utilize the power, whereas in democracy, the power is to be distributed. That is why democracy is sometimes defined as:

> Government by the people; that form of government in which the sovereign power resides in the people as a whole, and is exercised either directly by them ... or by officers elected by them.
>
> – *Oxford English Dictionary*

> Democracy is not majority rule: democracy is diffusion of power, representation of interests, and recognition of minorities.
>
> – Roper 1989: 93

> Democracy is a political system in which different groups are legally entitled to compete for power and in which institutional power holders are elected by the people and are responsible to the people. – Vanhannen 1997: 31

DEFINITION 3 [FROM THE PERSPECTIVE OF LIBERTY, EQUALITY AND FRATERNITY]

As the democracy is, still now, regarded as the highest form of government, naturally, it is expected that a democratic state must prevail the notion of liberty, equality and fraternity. From this perspective, democracy is defined as:

> A definition of the ideal: Government by the people, where liberty, equality and fraternity are secured to the greatest possible degree and in which human capacities are developed to the utmost, by means including free and full discussion of common problems and interests. – Pennock 1979: 6

In a democracy important public decisions on questions of law and policy depend, directly or indirectly, upon public opinion formally expressed by citizens of the community, the vast bulk of it have equal political rights (Weale 1999: 14).

DEFINITION 4 [FROM THE PERSPECTIVE OF ELECTION]

After population explosion, it is very rare to find out any country in the world where the citizens have been participating directly in administration through democracy. That is why election plays an important role to implement the representative form of democracy. From this aspect, democracy means:

> The competitive electoral context, with several political parties organizing the alternatives that face the voters, is the identifying property of the contemporary democratic process. ... Democratic systems are ... characterized by competitive elections in which most citizens are eligible to participate. – Powell 1982: 3

DEFINITION 5 [FROM THE PERSPECTIVE OF PARTICIPATION]

In the introductory paragraph, it has been mentioned that democracy is an ideal concept but it has practical application. Through the practice it will get perfection. For this reason active participation whether in direct or indirect form is necessary. That is why it is said that a "democratic regime" is:

> first and foremost a set of procedural rules for arriving at collective decisions in a way which accommodates and facilitates the fullest possible participation of interested parties.
>
> – Bobbio 1987: 7

DEFINITION 6 [FROM THE PERSPECTIVE OF RESOLVING CONFLICTS]

> Democracy is a form of institutionalization of continual conflicts ... and of uncertainty, of subjecting all interests to uncertainty.... .
>
> – Przeworski 1986: 14

This definition of democracy is, actually, emphasizing on the power of appeasing the conflicts, among the different interests exposed by the citizens of a state through democracy.

DEFINITION 7 [FROM THE PERSPECTIVE OF ACCOUNTABILITY]

Though it has been said that freedom is one of the vital conditions of democracy, the rulers not absolutely free to do anything as they will; they are actually, obligated to the common general public. From this point, it has been said:

> In democracy, the rulers must be modern political democracy is a system of governance in which rulers are held accountable for their actions in the public realm by citizens, acting indirectly

through the competition and cooperation of their elected representatives. – Schmitter and Karl 1991: 4

Democrats are committed to rule by the people. They insist that no aristocrat, monarch, philosopher, bureaucrat, expert, or religious leader has the right, in virtue of such status, to force people to accept a particular conception of their proper common life (Shapiro 1999: 29).

Democracy provides opportunities for

1. effective participation,
2. equality in voting,
3. gaining enlightened understanding,
4. exercising final control (by the people over the agenda), and
5. inclusion of adults.

The political institutions necessary to pursue these goals are:

1. elected officials,
2. free, fair and frequent elections,
3. freedom of expression,
4. alternative sources of information,
5. associational autonomy, and
6. inclusive citizenship. – Dahl 1998: 85

Final Domains of Responsibility

Though the concept of democracy is as old as the concept of human civilization, from the definitions of democracy mentioned above, it is clear that some more domains of responsibilities should be added. So, the final domains of responsibilities are as follows:

i. freedom or sovereignty of the people,
ii. free and fare elections,
iii. basic human rights,
iv. authority,

v. equality,
vi. due process of law,
vii. opposition,
viii. nationalism
ix. values of tolerance, pragmatism, cooperation and compromise,
x. influence of civil society, and
xi. education.

FREEDOM OR SOVEREIGNTY OF THE PEOPLE

The relationship between democracy and freedom is so intimate that they seem to be interchangeable. However, it should not be forgotten that the democracy is a set of idea which is a principle about freedom, i.e. the field of domain is freedom and democracy is under this domain. After a long and thorough continuous practice, democracy may be institutionalized for freedom. Now arise a few questions:

1. Why freedom is so important in democracy?
2. What type of freedom is essential for democracy?
3. Is there any limitation in democratic freedom?

Freedom, especially intellectual freedom, in any form, whatever it may be, is very important, because man being rational, he has an intrinsic value. He should deserve the dignity of his intellectual choices which are expressed through the application of his freedom of choices. It is necessary from other perspective also. Human being, though tries his best to make an adjustment with the nature in order to survive, it may be possible, in anytime, the entire human species is in a crisis and at that time, the unique, i.e. free thinking, can show the way how to resolve the crisis. However, democracy demands the freedom of choice as well as the freedom of expression of thoughts. What type of freedom is essential in democracy will be clear, if it is contrasted with the notion of enlightenment, because without any freedom of thought, enlightenment of society is impossible. It is true that most of the human beings do not want to bring any kind of enlightenment, as it is the emergence from self-imposed non-age, i.e. the inability to use one's own understanding without the guidance of other. It is self-imposed, because their causes do not lie in the lack of understanding, but in indecision and lack of courage to use one's own mind without the guidance of others. In fact, if a book is available for gathering knowledge, a pastor for conscience, a doctor for treatment and so on; we need not go for any kind of free thinking if we can just pay. But there were some rare persons, from time immemorial, who have failed to keep them away from thinking with the help of others and bring enlightenment in the society. It is noteworthy that such rare persons could think by going ahead of their time what common general public failed to realize. That is why, freedom of thought is acceptable, but it should be in accordance with the acceptability of the future generation. However, in the case of democracy, there is no absolute freedom, because in that case, there is a probability of the failure of the total system. Only those types of freedom are acceptable which never collapse the whole democratic system but uplift it.

FREE AND FARE ELECTIONS

As far as the constitutional-based representative democracy is concerned, the roles of judiciary, election process and administration are very important. Fair election is possible, if and only if, the citizens are conscious about their basic rights. But practically, it has been noticed that a large number of people in developing countries are not conscious about their basic human rights laid down in their constitution. There are rights, there are laws, there are rules, but these are only in paper. Seldom steps are taken by any country to apply these forces into the practical lives of the citizens. Winning an election is practically about that particular mathematical calculation where the willingness of 49 per cent citizens is ignored. When any dispute regarding election process arises, sometimes it has been observed, due to the long run process of judicial system, justice is not only delayed but also distracted in such a way that it seems that laws are for the riches. Furthermore, due to the advent of huge technological progress, life fast moving. Everyone is carving for the material comforts only. Anything whatever it may be, will be valueable if and only if it promotes the material comfort. Any hindrance in getting these material comforts is intolerable. So, being a responsible citizen, it is our duty to be the part of a free and fare election.

BASIC HUMAN RIGHTS

It has been mentioned earlier that we should be conscious about our basic rights in order to participate in a free and fare election. In fact, many democratic thinkers such as John Locke argue for certain rights which should never be given up or taken away from the masses, because in that case, people may not join the larger society or government, that is to say a democratic government will not be formed. However, if a government does try to take them away from their rights, the people are justified in revolting to change the government. Again, any democratic system of government, where more than one party is involved, the government is formed by only a party that has been elected, through a free and fare election. In general, before winning the election, each party makes its a promises about their future destinations to the masses through its manifesto. But, there may be a possibility of despotism by the elected government also. That is why some fundamental human rights are reserved in the constitution. In the Indian constitution, the citizens are empowered to enjoy the following basic human rights:

i. Right to equality – Articles 14, 15 and 16.

ii. Right to six freedoms – Article 19.

   a. Freedom of speech and expression.
   b. Freedom to assemble peacefully and without arms.
   c. Freedom to form associations or unions.
   d. Freedom to move freely throughout the territory of India.
   e. Freedom to reside and settle in any part of the territory of India.
   f. Freedom to practise any profession or carry on any occupation, trade or business.

iii. Right to life and personal liberty – Articles 20, 21 and 22.
iv. Right to freedom of religion – Articles 25, 26, 27 and 28.
v. Cultural and educational rights – Articles 29 and 30.
vi. Right to property – Article 31 (the 44th amendment has deleted this right and re-enacted it in Article 300A, as constitutional right).
vii. Right against exploitation – Articles 23 and 24.
viii. Right to constitutional remedies – Article 32.

AUTHORITY

In case of constitution-based representative form of democratic government, the role of elected authorities is very important; otherwise, no state can be an ideal state. Presently, democracy is depended on various parties, amongst which one of them is elected for a certain time to govern the state. In that duration, it should be the duties of the winning party to develop the state in those ways what they have already committed in their manifesto. But practically, it has been observed that every party after winning the election fails to keep its promises which they have made in their manifesto and follows some tricky ways so that they could win the election again and again. Now the point is: how should we overcome this situation? We may, in this regard, flashback what Plato said in his book *Republic* long days ago. Though Plato did not talk about anything directly regarding the ideal state, he, at the time of discussing the justice, stated about the ideal state where each of the individual person would occupy his own position and perform his own duties imposed upon him, following the laws and orders. He strongly believed that such a type of state is the trademark where justice in true sense could be established.

The structure of an ideal state for Plato is hinged upon the rulers who are bound to follow the law. In this connection, Plato mentioned that the philosophers should take the charge of rulers. Apparently, it looks absurd. But, there is a deep meaning in what

Plato thought. In fact, the aim of a philosopher is to search for the knowledge of the ultimate; that is why it is possible only for a philosopher, to make a real judgement in any situation after considering it from different angles. Again, a philosopher, being the seeker of truth, must be free from any kind of prejudices, pettiness and narrow ideas. Furthermore, as he searches for the ultimate good, naturally, it would be good for all. Plato also believed that the rulers mind should be free from any kind of selfishness, partiality and sordid ideas, but full of love for truth. That is why he preferred the rulers to keep themselves away from family life; there should be nothing which could distract their mind. For these reasons, Plato was convinced to say that there would be no respite from evil, unless the philosophers become the rulers. However, we may not fully agree with him, but we cannot deny that Plato's scheme bears the permanent value which should not be missed any time. There must be a gap between what is ideal and what is real; we should try our best to follow the ideal the best possible way. So, the authorities should be conscious about their destination, they should be free from any kind of biasness and do their best, at least for the future generations. Because, all of us are undoubtedly obliged, what we have been doing at present, to our beloved future generation.

EQUALITY

In the *Cambridge Advanced Learners Dictionary*, the term equality has been defined as "the right of different groups of people to have a similar social position and receive the same treatment, equality between the sexes, racial equality". It includes five separate types of equality:

- political equality,
- equality before the law,
- equality of opportunity,
- economic equality, and
- equality of respect or social equality.

Though there are many forms through which the political

equality is expressed, it mainly stands for the equality at the ballot box, equality in the ability to be elected to public office, and equality of political influence. Equality before the law is one of the most powerful rights of the citizens in a representative form of government. Each citizen of a country may be influential from the perspective of his political power or of his/her economic power, but when he/she is moved to the court he/she is given the same status as like what a simple citizen is being paid by the court. That is why the depiction of justice is usually shown a blindfolded woman holding a scale. The scale is, in fact, the indication that the issues will be weighed on the basis of law; the blindfold indicates that there will be no scope of weighing through any unfair means. It is a fact that a democratic-representative form of government will be ceased to exist if the judiciary is corrupt. Equality of opportunity signifies the social stratification and mobility systems where it is expected that every individual in the society can move up or down within the class or status system depending on the ability of the individual, no artificial barrier keeps away any person from achieving his/her success on the basis of his/her constant hard work. Any kind of artificial barriers such as race, gender, religion, ethnic, national origin, so on and so forth can never be a subject of special treatment for a citizen whoever he/she may be. In the case of equality from the perspective of economy, though some thinkers talk about the equality of income, it seems to be ideal. From the practical point of view, it can be said that a citizen must be guaranteed of his/her minimum level of income security which makes him/her to be an active citizen. Though it is really difficult to define what is equality of respect or social equality as all humans by default are the subjects to be given the same status. However, from the perspective of Immanuel Kant, it can be said that no human being should be categorized from the perspective of his/her caste or race or nation or religion, because all human beings have equal intrinsic value. We should pay respect to all humans as they are humans, that's all.

DUE PROCESS OF LAW

We all are aware of the maxim related to justice – justice delayed is justice denied. It means, if the legal redress or equitable relief to an injured party is available, but has not been executed due to long legal process, its effectiveness will be blunted. In fact, the party has failed to get justice, not because of the law but because of the implementation of the law in due time. Surprisingly, in India there are 3.7 million cases pending in courts for over ten years. So, it is the main duty of the authorities as well as citizens, in order to save democracy, to focus on the matter that justice should not be delayed.

OPPOSITION

Opposition, which is one of the necessary conditions of democracy, is deactivated just after the announcement of the result of the election either by the opposition leaders or by the force of the winning party whose representatives are in the government. A leader of any party, who is also one of the responsible parts of the implementation of the democracy, at present, is known not for his work but for his corruptions. However, in order to do the best for the state, there must be a room for opposition. Without having any criticism nothing can reach to its perfection. In fact, political tolerance should be cultivated by all the leaders. If the aim of all the leaders is the development of the country, the opposition and the ruling party should act as complementary to each other.

NATIONALISM

Though nationalism is a modern concept, following Anthony D. Smith's opening statement on the Warwick Debates, it can be defined as:

> ... an ideological movement for the attainment of autonomy, unity and identity of human population, some of whose members conceive it to constitute an actual or potential "nation". A "nation" in turn (is defined) as a named human population

> sharing an historic territory, common myths and memories, a mass, public culture, a single economy and common rights and duties for all members.

From this definition, it is clear that the idea of nationalism is meaningless, if it is not certified with the idea of a nation. Some European scholars think nationalism emerges out of the modernization based on capitalism after the Industrial Revolution, especially, in Europe, when nationalism has been working as a force or power, all the members of a particular nation started to feel their uniqueness and superiority over the other nations. Naturally, the colonial ideology of nationalism, based on materialistic approach, leads to a competition among the different nations.

But as the history of *Homo sapiens*, nationalism has its own historical naval point which reflects, it can never be emerged out of only materialistic approaches as the colonial ideology strongly believed; what M.K. Gandhi in his entire life tried to prove to the whole world. Gandhi focused on the spiritual nature of human being in order to realize what nationalism was, especially from the Indian sagacious intellectual perspective. Human being has an aesthetic sense, a feeling-sensibility and an insight into the nature of what is good and what is bad. These are not just physical activities; these are all expressions of the real man – of the spirit or soul present in him. Being an ardent follower of monism, i.e. keeping belief in the supreme reality of God, he was firmly convinced that human beings were the expression of God. Naturally, the Gandhian concept of nationalism was not only based on *ahiṁsā* and love, the two soul forces of human being, but also acted as the kinetic power of nationalism in true sense. This type of spiritualistic nationalism has two aspects – broad and narrow. At the time of the freedom movement, which is from the narrow aspect of nationalism, the Indians fought against the British after being a *satyāgrahī*. Passive resistance was the sole weapon which was used against the British Raj in accordance with *ahiṁsā* and love. Unlike colonial-cum-materialistic approach, Gandhi thought that the nations might be different, but we should not forget that human beings were the same from the perspective of inner soul force which is full of love and the expression of God. From this perspective of Gandhian nationalism, i.e. from the broad aspect of nationalism, there will be no competition among the different nations, there will be one and only one nation of *Homo sapiens* based on *ahiṁsā* and love.

VALUES OF TOLERANCE, PRAGMATISM, COOPERATION AND COMPROMISE

A state whether it is governed in the form of constitution-based representative government or not, we should keep in mind that a state is not just a machine which will run following some mechanical law, rather it may be taken as organism as a whole where the laws, judicial systems are the sensible parts of that organ. Democracy has a destination. It aims to provide the citizens such types of governance where no citizens can think that he/she is actually deprived of the state. In order to do this, we the citizens including the authorities, cultivate some good qualities such as the power of tolerance, accepting the decision made by the state following the situation, in a larger sense to give full cooperation, compromise as well as commitment. Among these good qualities, the term tolerance signifies the acceptance of another person believing or doing something that one believes to be wrong. Religious tolerance is one of the most obvious cases. If, I am certain that my way is the only way through which one leads to salvation, then it will be difficult to handle the situation. Being a responsible citizen, I should give more attention to the view of the others, especially, to the view of opposition as it has been pointed out earlier. If any inconsistency is found in the view of the opposition, it must be defended on the basis of strong arguments, not on the basis of any biased opinion. Without tolerance, democracy cannot work.

INFLUENCE OF CIVIL SOCIETY

Though democracy, still now, is regarded as the best form of governing a state, the role of civil society can never be ignored.

In fact, the notion of civil society is as old as the idea of state. Immanuel Kant, in this regard, remarked that a civil society must be governed in the principle of the intrinsic value of the human beings – no people should be treated as means but as an end. Civil society, in fact, acts as the critical-mirror-cum-conscience of the elected government. As the democracy depends on many parties, amongst them one and only one party is liable to form the government through election, naturally, there must be some hidden agenda which may be harmful for the future generations. The ordinary, simple citizens will not be capable to guess such hidden agendas. Only a civil society has the power to realize such agendas and to make the general citizen conscious. Again, if a state suddenly faces natural calamities such as an earth quake, pandemic and so on, the civil society is responsible in giving suggestions to the administrative authorities. Not only that, if an elected democratic government starts practising autocracy, then at once, the civil society has the power to warn the government and throw off from its position through a revolution. However, twentieth century's Italian neo-Marxist political thinker Antonio Gramsci and German philosopher and sociologist Jurgen Habermas in their books *Selection from the Prison Notebooks* (1971) and *The Structural Transformation of the Public Sphere* (1991) respectively, analysed the concept of "civil society" as a specific institution of the state. It is, in fact, that "superstructure" comprising of family, school and church. It is an instrument of getting apparent consent of the common people for the state as an emblem of justice. Civil society works as a support-giving mechanism in the smooth running of a democratic state.

EDUCATION

In democracy, whether it is constitutional or not, participation of each citizen is necessary. A citizen can take part in the democracy either from the perspective of an elected member, i.e. the ruler, or from the perspective of an ordinary citizen. A citizen whether he is in the position of a ruler or not, he must have the minimum knowledge about the pros and cons through which he can express his choice in the various domains of democracy such as election, policy making and so on. For getting the minimum knowledge, every citizen should know how to read, write and calculate. Education and only education can make a good citizen. If the citizens are educated then democracy will reach its ideal state within a stipulated time. However, it should be note worthy that the designation of the term education is not as same as the term learning or literate. An illiterate person may be educated from the perspective of transcendental life. That is why Swami Vivekananda used to say that education is the manifestation which is already in man. Rabindranath Tagore also believed that perfect education helped man to be uplifted to the stage of higher self (*baro ami*) from lower self (*choto ami*). Nevertheless, there is no contradiction between education and learning. The term learning is actually associated with the training. Unless and until the citizens are properly trained how to utilize their intellectual capacities, they can never participate actively in democracy. For this reason, John Locke, Jean-Jacques Rousseau and John Stuart Mill wrote treatises on education that tied their political theories to the need for an educated populace. Any illiterate citizen, in a democratic state, is just like a child who depends on his guardian. Literacy generates that power through which a citizen can demand his constitutional rights, can judge which party is the best, can take part at the time of policy making, can think for their own development, can separate the proximate gain and approximate gain, can understand the need of education for the future generation, can realize the national unity as highest than the unity from the perspective of community or religion, can plan for a bright future, can help the government being the part of a good civil society and so on.

These are some of the domains where we should pay our constant responsibilities in order to continue the democratic form of government. It is true that we never reach the ideal form of democracy, but we should not neglect the ideal.

References

Aristotle, 1995, *Politics*, New York: Oxford University Press.

Bobbio, Norberto, 1987, *The Future of Democracy: A Defence of the Rules of the Game*, New York: Polity.

Dahl, Robert A., 1998, *On Democracy*, New Haven, CT : Yale University Press.

Pennock, J. Roland, 1979, *Democratic Political Theory*, Princeton, NJ: Princeton University Press.

Powell, G., 1982, *Bingham: Contemporary Democracies,* Cambridge, MA: Harvard University Press.

Przeworski, Adam, 1986, "Some Problems in the Study of the Transition to Democracy", in *Transitions from Authoritarian Rule: Prospects for Democracy* [Part III], ed. Guillermo, O'Donnell, C. Phillipe, Schmitter, and Laurence Whitehead, pp. 47-63, Baltimore, MD: Johns Hopkins University Press.

Roper, Jon, 1989, *Democracy and Its Critics: Anglo-American Democratic Thought in the Nineteenth Century,* Winchester, MA: Unwin Hyman.

Shapiro, Ian, 1999, *Democratic Justice*, New Haven, CT: Yale University Press.

Schmitter, C. Philippe and Karl Terry Lynn, 1991, "What Democracy Is ... And Is Not", *Journal of Democracy* (Summer), pp. 75-88.

Vanhannen, Tatu, 1997, *Prospects of Democracy: A Study of 172 Countries*, New York: Routledge.

Weale, Albert, 1999, *Democracy*, New York: St. Martin's Press.

7

Created Leadership, Power and Ethics

A Critical Analysis

Tapan Kumer De

Introduction

LEADERSHIP includes power. Leadership without power is impossible in present democratic system. The question is how to exercise the power for the benefit of the society? It is thought that the power must be used in accordance with the concept of ethics. A leader must have to follow the norms set by the concept of ethics at the time of exercising power. In democratic field the ethics of responsibility must be followed. If any leader fails to do his job following the concept of ethics of responsibility, he is considered as a leader without a goal. Traditional leadership, charismatic leadership, legal-rational leadership as divided by Max Weber are successful leadership in democracy as they all intend to follow the norms of the ethics of responsibility. At present, a new trend of leadership emerged in the end part of the last century in India. The trend is to handover the power to the future generations without listening to the opinion of other followers. This new kind of leadership is in question while exercising their power which they have inherited from their predecessors. They generally fail to grasp the importance of ethics in politics. Rather, they show their interests to exercise the power according to their will. They use to force not only the followers of their ideology but also use the official mechanism to establish their supremacy and they do not think that the general people are the ultimate source of power due to lack of experience. As they hold the chair in their offices without any struggle, they have no capability to realize the value of political struggle to come to power. Power comes to them as an inherited property and they begin to exercise it as the property holders, not as true leaders. In this paper, I am going to analyse the concept of leadership and power in connection with the concept of ethics. It will be shown that the new trend of leadership, i.e. created leadership, is not fit for the democratic countries. A leader who is selected directly as a leader without any discussion or election but following the theory of parachutism[1] is called a created leader. The creation is made without cultivating any inner quality in the selected persons rather they are selected on the basis of the close relationship with those in power. So their dedication, action and motivation are always in question.

The word "leadership" comes from the word "leader". A leader is one who leads his community or followers. A good leader, especially in democracy, acquires power through his leadership. Naturally leadership comes first and the power follows it. Power (political power) is not the essential quality of a leader. A leader may or may not have power but he enjoys leadership.

[1] 'Parachutisms' is a theory that indicates a new process to make a non-political person a political leader. Generally a person comes down from air to the land by parachut. The word 'Parachut' is used in a different scene. When a leader introduces his family members as a leader, who has no connection with politics, is surely using the mechanism of parachut. Now a days, particularly in India, the parachut process is used by various political parties to create a non-leader from non-political family members. The process of creating leader is being theorized here by the author and the word parachutism is used to indicate this process.

Mahatma Gandhi is the fittest example in this connection. According to Louis Fisher, a famous writer from England, "His power was nil, but authority enormous". Gandhiji never became the prime minister of India or the president of India. He consciously kept himself away from the power circle, yet he had Himalayan leadership and he was able to lead the masses in correct path. But at present, it is believed by the leaders that power is essential for perfect leadership. Without power, no leader can be treated as a successful leader.

In Gandhian concepts, leadership must be followed by power. But the reverse is believed at present. It is believed that power must be followed by the leadership. Hence the relation between the concept of ethics and the concept of leadership has been completely changed from what it was believed earlier. Power-centric leadership also changes its ethics from time to time. Not only that, it intentionally creates new ethical concepts for its sustenance in the circle of power.

Now, let us come to the point of leadership. What leadership is the main focusing point at this juncture? Glenn D. Paige in his *The Scientific Study of Political Leadership* explains the important characteristics of a leader. There he says that there are so many dimensions to a leader: leadership as decision and persuasion, implementation or creative imagination, class dominant influence by example, skilful management of social relations, creative brutality based upon hostiles against out group enemies, revolutionary explanation and consolidation of class interest, satisfaction of follower needs, task performance, slave or master of circumstances, emotional exchange, etc. (1977: 64-65). The entire qualities mentioned above regarding leadership indicates various dimensions of leadership. Leadership is the ability to decide assignments for the interest of the party or government or country and at the same time to influence others to do the same with a strong belief. Without this ability of decision-making procedure a leader will not be a successful one and the concept of leadership will appear as a doom. A political leader must have the ability of creative imagination. A leader can anticipate the invisible states of affairs of his followers. Skilful management of social relations is an essential quality of a leader, as a leader has to deal with public problems. A good leader must have the ability to distinguish the appearance of the opponent from that of his followers. It is thought that each and every goal man has reached with the execution of originality – that has creative brutality based upon hostilities against out-group enemies – is also an important factor of a good leader. Without the power of execution of qualitative brutality, a leader will not be a successful one. Following Lenin, Paige says:

> The art of the politician and the correct understanding by the communist of his own tasks, consists in the correct appraisal of the condition and the moment when the vanguard of the proletariat can successfully seize power; when it will be able, during and after this, to obtain sufficient support from sufficiently broad sections of the working class and the non-proletarian working masses; when he will, after that, be able to support, strengthen, and broaden his rule, educating, teaching and attracting wider and wider masses of the labouring population. – 1977: 66

Political leadership, as I have mentioned earlier, depends on the relation between the leader and the followers. The fruitful relation indicates that the leader has the ability to satisfy the needs of his followers. To satisfy the needs of his followers a leader must have to play the role of a slave or the role of a master as situation demands. In a comprehensive way, it can be said that the political leadership is a complex concept having various kinds of positive and negative qualities. The situation of a leader may be compared with a battlefield where the leader must have to fight for the benefit of his followers and to defeat his opponent by conquering his power.

What is ethics? Generally the word ethics indicates the sumtotal of criteria to be used to judge an action performed by a human being. An action is good when it, in accordance with the principle of morality ethics, deals with values. Which is morally good and bad is addressed by ethics. The action of a person is judged with the help of moral standards. The terms ethics and morality are interdependent. We commonly refer to ethical judgement of moral principle to be applied to judge the action of a human being. There are different theories of ethics which are important in the field of philosophy such as egoism, hedonism, Kantianism, utilitarianism, contractualism, religion and distributive justice. Kantianism is important to judge the action of a political leader. Whether a man is used as means, instead of ends, is a matter of judgement in Kantianism. According to Kant, nothing in the world-indeed – nothing even beyond the world – can possibly be conceived which could be called good without qualification except a goodwill. Intelligence, wit, judgement and other talents of the mind, however they may be named, or courage, resoluteness and perseverance as qualities of temperament are, doubtlessly in many respects, good and desirable. But they can become extremely bad and harmful if the will, which is to make use of these gifts of nature and which in its special constitution is called character, is not good. Power, riches, honour, even health, general well-being and the contentment with one's condition which is called happiness, make for pride and even arrogance if there is no goodwill to correct their influence on the mind and on its principles of action so as to make it universally conformable to its end. It need hardly be mentioned that the sight of a being adorned with no feature of a pure and goodwill, yet enjoying uninterrupted prosperity [i.e. anyone like Faust] can never give pleasure to a rational impartial observer. Thus, the goodwill seems to constitute the indispensable condition even of worthiness to be happy (Kant 1996: 9). Kant here wants to establish the concept of good in metaphysical sense. On the other hand, utilitarian beliefs are in a different way. Maximum good or maximum people is the main theory of utilitarianism. Rawl's distributive justice also demands equal opportunity for all. In political field, it is demand that ethics of responsibility must be there. In this paper I want to show the compatibility with ethics of the concept of leadership as which types of leadership follow the rules of ethics by overcoming the conflict of interest.

Now take the point-leadership and ethics. Leadership must have some qualities to follow the norms of ethics for the good of the society. Leadership is a quality by which a person or a group of persons able to make others do something which they do not want to do or do not like to do. The quality mentioned here is nothing but the power to be exercised. A leader must have the power to motivate his followers to a thing or things for the interest of the others. In a nutshell, leadership is a social process which binds the leader with his followers in the thread of the ethics of responsibility and offers the scope to the leader to make understand his ideal to his followers and ideologically forces them to render their services to the society according to the demand of him.

Power is also an important phenomenon in this respect as the concept of leadership entails the concept of power. So it is necessary to explain the concept of power in this juncture. Let us see how the concept of power was defined by famous writers.

Robert Michel, a famous sociologist, viewed the emergence of the mass party in the early part of twentieth century fostered within the organization a power which is structural elitist and possesses its own particular logic (Rye 2014: 1). These power-centric political organizations, political parties are engaged in political struggle to hold the power to dominate the others. It is nothing but a fighting of the relatively weak against the so-called powerful, i.e. only the power holder to have the power by defeating the opponents. To win the struggle and to gain the power to dominate the masses, a strong, elected and professional leadership is required. The legitimate use of power with the main aim to do good to others is the central thought of my paper. In my paper I am just going to dwell upon the concept of "leadership and ethics" to show the right path to use the political power by the various types of leaders.

Undoubtedly, there is a deep relation between leadership and power. According to Panebianco "power is an unequal exchange relation in which leader seeks freedom to act and members seek material and solidarity benefit" (Rye 2014: 16). Panebianco explained the power from a different point of view. He did not believe that power is a fixed or frozen set of relation or hierarchy; rather, to him, power is a changing and evolving resource. Political parties are exercising power to ensure the benefit of the masses. There is no question about the matter that in democracy power is like a motto to help to run political parties to develop their policies and aims uninterruptedly. According to Panebianco for leaders,

> to exercise power they must conversely submit themselves to the power of members. The power of a leader can therefore never be absolute or arbitrary .... It is limited by the necessity to interact with followers and it can only be properly exercised if members themselves are satisfied and content. – Ibid.

Let us consider the second concept of power as defined by Hannah Arendt. "Power", she writes, corresponds to the human ability not just to act but to act in concert. Power is never the property of an individual; it belongs to a group and remains in existence only so long as the group keeps together. When we say of somebody that he is "in power" we actually refer to his being empowered by a certain number of people to act in their name. The moment the group, from which the power originated to begin with (*potestas in populo*, without a people or group there is no power), disappears, "his power" also vanishes, the people's support lends power to the institutions of a country, and this support is but the continuation of the consent that brought the laws into existence to begin with. Under conditions of representative government the people are supposed to rule those who govern them. All political institutions are manifestations and materializations of power; they petrify and decay as soon as the living power of the people ceases to uphold them. This is what Madison meant when he said "all governments rest on opinion", a word no less true for the various forms of monarchy than for democracies (Lukes 1974: 28).

We can say that Panebianco theoretically explained the

relationship between the power holder and the source of the power. In democracy, people are the source of power and leaders of political parties are the power holders. It is theoretically true that the relationship is equal. If a leader fails to satisfy the need of the masses he will not be able to win the next election to enjoy the power. So the leaders of the political parties always try to show the equal status of the power relation.

It is said that the concept of power is not static, it is dynamic in nature. Power may be designated as coercive force, i.e. power over or it may indicate a special kind of capacity of the power holder to shape the power according to his own logic. According to Morris, "power is always a concept referring to an ability, capacity or dispositional property" (2006: 13). So to him, power is a dispositional property which refers to the capacity or to the ability to do something freely or to have the capacity to control or dominate the followers.

Morris again says:

> Although the term "power" may be used in several distinct contexts, meaning something different each time, it remains that power needs to be understood in all circumstances as something that is employed to effect things rather than to affect things.
>
> – Ibid.: 30

Morris clearly explains that power is a tool to be used by the power holder to do something according to his or her wish. The use of power depends upon the capacity of the person concerned. A person may have power without capacity to use it. In this case, it can be said that this person cannot use his power properly to make it more useful. On the other hand, a person with the capacity or skill to use power will enjoy more freedom to do something or to bring changes in the society by using it.

The other concept of power, i.e. "power coercion" or "power over" is also explained thoroughly. The concept of "power over" comes from the conflict and coercion. Power always generates conflicts between two persons or two groups to hold the power. Let us see what has been told by Dahl in a form of formula to explain the concept of power over. The formula is formed in this way:

> *A* has power over *B* to the extent that he can get *B* to do something that *B* would not otherwise do. – Rye 2014: 34

The formula has three dimensions. Power always needs two parties to be exercised. One party will exercise the power over the other to fulfil his interest. The first one will use the power over the second. The second party will follow the command of the power holder.

This theory was modified again by Bachrach and Baratz in 1917 who argued that the power had a second face in which same (usually elite) actors exercised power in a less obviously visible or confrontational way to prevent the interest of others from being addressed thus protecting their own position (ibid.). It may be said that *A* has power over *B*, i.e. *A* exercises power over *B* in a different way, i.e. *A* may influence *B* to act according to his desire or *A* may shape the attitude or motive of *B* for a particular purpose or *A* may determine the way he wants to do the job by *B*. Lukes says to indicate the kind of power in this way:

> So I conclude that the two-dimensional view of power involves a qualified critique of the behavioural focus of the first view (I say qualified because it is still assumed that non-decision making is a form of decision-making) and it allows form consideration of the ways in which decision are prevented from being taken on potential issues over which there is on observable conflict of (subjective) interests, seen as embodied in express policy preferences and sub-political grievances. – 1974: 24-25

The concept of interest comes into the arena of discussion on power over. The power holder always tries to exercise his power over the followers keeping in mind the interest. The interest may be in connection with the political party or may be his personal interest. Here the concept of ethics comes into force. It is desirable that the power holder should always exercise his power over others for the greater interest of the society. Utilitarian theory approves such kinds of actions which are capable to bring happiness for the maximum numbers. If any decision taken by the power holder helps the majority of the society, then his decision will be ethically approved according to the utilitarian point of view. Obviously a value judgement will be there at the time of taking political decision by political leaders.

Scholars like Lukes think that there is a problem of interest. Luke says that the way in which people act and perceive their own desires might be contrary to their interest as defined in such a way (1974: 24). It may be said that Lukes here wants to introduce a mere objective way of understanding interest. It is called objective because the concept of interest in connection with power over is predetermined and pre-shaped. But we have to keep in mind that the concept of objective interest as explained by Lukes will appear more problematic as a kind of false consciousness is associated with the concept of objective interest. The conflict of interest is also explained in a different way. A question may arise in this connection: whether the power over can be exercised by the power holder on the followers in the real interest of the followers. Here conflict between the preferences of the power holder and followers comes into focus. The power holder may influence the followers in favour of his own interest but motivate them as the interest of the followers. That means the power holder shows his attitude at the time of fulfilling his interest in a different manner that he is giving priority to the interest of the followers.

One of the leading thinkers, Petter Digeser explains the matter from a different point of view. According to Digeser, "the power forges subjects, imbues and creates social practices and forms of discourage that sustained politics". Thus, power produces interest and engenders desires into which individuals are forged (1992: 989).

Now we want to give a brief explanation on the concept of "false consciousness". The meaning of the concept of false consciousness is an attitude in which a person is purposefully motivated to perceive a phenomenon from a different point of view where the actual nature of the phenomenon does not reveal. According to Michel J. Thomson, false consciousness is that

> it is locked into a routinized pattern of cognition that disables critical cognitive and epistemic capacities and naturalizes the dominant ideas and values that legitimate prevailing power relations and interest. – 2014: 2

So, false consciousness is the by-product of the concept of interest. It is related with the present situation of leadership.

The leader's interest may be sectional and thereby generates radicals in the society for holding the power and to snatch it by the opponent. Actually in political leadership, power is used as an esteemed property. The collective goals or even the values, which lie behind them may be the outcome of a negotiated order built on conflict between parties holding different power, are ignored, since for persons power assumes the prior existence of collectively goals (ibid.: 30).

So, the concept of interest is problematic because we fail to assume that all interests are reflected directly in present action. It is also difficult to understand whose interest is being undertaken at the time of exercising power by the power holder. Lukes points out that there is a conflict between the preferences of *A* and *B*, but that *A*'s preferences are *B*'s real interest, to this there are two possible responses:

1. that *A* might exercise "short-time power" over *B* (with an observable conflict of subjective interest), but that if and when *B* recognizes his real interest, the power relation ends; it is self-annihilating, or
2. that all or most forms of attempted or successful control by *A* over *B*, when *B* objects or resists, constituted a violation of *B*'s autonomy; that *B* has a real interest in his own autonomy; so that such an exercise of power cannot be in *B*'s real interest. Clearly the first of these responses of open to misuse

> by seeming to provide a paternalist license for tyranny; while the second furnishes an anarchist defense against it, collapsing all or most cases of influence into power.
>
> – Lukes 1974: 36

Max Weber, one of the famous sociologists and philosophers, in his masterwork *Economy and Society*, classifies leadership in political field into three types – charismatic, traditional and legal-rational. All of them are corresponding to a brand of leadership functioning in the contemporary society (2019: 37).

Charismatic Leadership

It is accepted that the concept of charismatic leadership was initiated by Saint Paul in the field of religion to inspire and motivate the Christian leaders for preaching of the religion all over the world, in a letter he wrote to the emerging Christian communities in the first century. It was demanded that all the Christian religious leaders have a divine gift to demonstrate the absolute authority of God. The divine power is called charisma. This power helps a religious leader to dominate a whole Christian community. No one has any kind of doubt in connection with the charismatic power of a religious leader but to accept his leadership without any question. As this leadership was granted as the command of God.

Max Weber at first took this theological concept of charismatic leadership and transformed it into a sociological one. From then it has become a convenience to use the concept of charismatic leadership to indicate a leader working in any field like politics, corporate sector and defence sector. Charismatic leadership points to an individual who possesses certain characters that make him amazing. This type of leader is not only able to lead his followers in an unquestionable way but actually holds the superior power of charisma to lead his people having different kinds of traits. The source of power of a charismatic leader is the enormous confidence and almost indestructible reliance of his followers on him.

Charismatic authority comes out of a person's extraordinary

personal qualities. And these extraordinary personal qualities help that leader to hold the power over his followers. A charismatic leader may exercise his power over the whole society or on only a specific group of a large society. Mahatma Gandhi, Gautama Buddha, Sri Chaitanya, Swami Vivekananda, Netaji Subhas Chandra Bose, Adolf Hitler and Martin Luther King Jr are the best examples of charismatic leadership. All these great personalities had God-gifted charisma and they applied their extraordinary power over their followers.

Charismatic authority can reside in a person who came to a position of leadership because of traditional or rational–legal authority. Over the centuries, several kings and queens of England and other European nations were charismatic individuals as well (while some were far from charismatic). A few US presidents –Washington, Lincoln, both Roosevelts, Kennedy, Reagan and, for all his faults, even Clinton – also were charismatic, and much of their popularity stemmed from various personal qualities that attracted the public and sometimes even the press. Ronald Reagan, for example, was often called "the Teflon president", because he was so loved by much of the public that accusations of ineptitude or malfeasance did not stick to him.

Weber clearly tells that charismatic authority in its pure form (i.e. when authority resides in someone solely because of the person's charisma and not because the person also has traditional or rational–legal authority) suffers from the disease of less stability than traditional authority or rational–legal authority. As it depends solely on the charisma of an individual the death of the person concerned is a great factor. With the death of a charismatic leader, his authority also dies as well. Although a charismatic leader's example may continue to inspire people long after his death, it is difficult for another leader to come along and command people's devotion as intensely. After the deaths of all the charismatic leaders named in the preceding paragraph, no one came close to replacing them in the hearts and minds of their followers.

Man is mortal. This universal and eternal truth forces a charismatic leader to recognize the untold truth which will happen in near future after his death. Generally, these people want to make a replacement of the same. They also think that the person who is going to be selected the future as leader may also have the charismatic qualities to lead the party in the same manner which he or she follows. From this anticipation of the charismatic leader the concept of the created leadership comes into existence. This selected leader may be a grown child of the present charismatic leader or someone else whom the charismatic leader knows, trusts and loves and has faith on him. The danger, of course, is that any new leader will lack sufficient charisma to have his authority accepted by the followers of the original charismatic leader. For this reason, Weber recognizes that charismatic authority ultimately becomes more stable when it advances into traditional or rational-legal authority. Transformation into traditional authority can happen when a charismatic leader's authority becomes accepted as residing in their bloodlines, so that their authority passes to their children and then to their grandchildren. Transformation into rational-legal authority occurs when a society ruled by a charismatic leader develops the rules and bureaucratic structures that we associate with a government. Weber used the term routinization of charisma to refer to the transformation of charismatic authority in either of these ways.

Second, traditional authority specifies the existence of a leading personality. The authority of this kind of leadership depends on the establishment of tradition or directive. While this leader is also a dominant personality, the prevailing order in society approves the command to rule. This type of leadership, however, is contemplative of everyday repetitive works and behaviour.

Third, legal-rational authority completely depends on the ground of laws. The power and the authority are clearly defined by the existing laws. The obedience of people is not based on the capacity or on the charisma of a leader but on the lawfulness and capability that procedures and laws confer upon him as authority. The present society needs this type of rationalization, as the complications of its various problems necessitate the appearance of a bureaucracy that embodies order and arrangement. This form of authority is a trademark of modern democracies as the power in such mode of rule is given to a leader through voting system. The rules for exercising that power are naturally set forth in a constitution or a charter or another written document that is well accepted by the sources of power. So it can be said that the rational–legal authority is an office-based authority. The role of a person is insignificant here.

The authority of the president of India or the authority of the prime minister of India or the authority of a chief minister of a state of India is a good example of such kind of leadership. All the leaders are elected for a certain duration to hold the power by holding the offices concerned. After the completion of the tenure the leaders leave their offices and the authority transfers to the next chair holders. This transfer is usually law-based and there is nothing to oppose it. It is the marvellous features of the modern democracy that the replacement of the office holders is happening through election. This process needs no revolution of bloodshed. As the authority in this type of leadership is elected, everyone has to show their obedience to that authority keeping aside all the differences.

A different kind of the concept of leadership is there in the political thought. The name of this leadership is transformational leadership. A transformational leader is a person who has the quality to stimulate and to transform his or her followers to achieve the goal of extraordinary outcomes. He or she shows interest to the necessity and the demand of his/her followers; such leaders change the attitude of their followers to look at old problems in a new way with a new hope to solve it to favour their interests. They have the capacity to stimulate, motivate and encourage their followers to engage in the given task with extra effort to achieve the goals set for the group concerned. The theory of transformational leadership is a kind of leadership that creates constructive change in the followers. They take care of each other's interests and at the same time dives for the interests of the section as a whole. This kind of leadership improves the inspiration, self-esteem and presentation of the followers taking the help of various mechanisms. These include connecting the followers' sense of identity and self to the plan and the cooperative individuality of the organization; being a role model for followers that inspires them and makes them attentive. It also throws challenges to the followers to take greater ownership in their work, and understanding the strengths and weaknesses of followers, so the leader can align his/her followers with tasks that enhance their performance.

Another kind of leadership also needs mention. This is called transactional leadership. It is also known as managerial leadership which focuses on the role of supervision, organization and group performance. Transactional leadership is a style of leadership where a leader promotes amenability of his followers through both rewards for better performance and punishments for the worst. Unlike transformational leadership, leaders using the transactional approach are not looking to change the future, they are looking to maintain the situation as it is. Any kind of alteration in this leadership is not desirable. Setting of rules and regulations is followed strictly and transactional leaders are there to pay attention to the works of their followers to make sure that everything is followed. Transactional leadership is more operative in getting definite tasks completed. It is a process-based model of leadership. Here the leaders are interested only in the process to be followed. Innovative ideas are not encouraged here.

Created Leadership

At present we find a new trend in Indian politics. This trend indicates the transformation of leadership in a democratic country like India. At present it goes from charismatic leadership to legal leadership and from legal leadership to creative one. Creative leadership means the creation of leadership. All over India we find in regional politics this trend is followed by each and every political party. Political parties are treated as property and they need to bear the flag of power by their family members. Most of the states are following the same tradition, such as Bihar, Uttar Pradesh and Tamil Nadu. The leaders of these states are chosen by the head of the parties keeping focus on the law of inheritance, such leaders are created not by their qualities but by their kinship. They are created leaders as they are not in the group of charismatic leaders. They have no charisma to lead a political party. They are not elected to be a ruler of traditional leadership. They are not a product of legal process and demands legal approval, basically they are created. The dominating power of the supreme authority of the party concerned forcefully projects the person as a leader coming from his or her home and forces the other members to be a follower of the same person without any question.

Created leadership is one of the forms of elitism in democracy. The word "elite" refers to a group of people who are powerful and capable of exercising their power guiding to their personal or sectional interests. This concept was popularized by Pareto and Mosca. According to Pareto,

> an elite consisted, primarily, of people whose ability and energy made them the most successful competitors as lawyers, politicians, entertainers, prostitutes, or any other social activity. – Norman 1992: 462

He again says that the most democratic regimes were governed by political elites, primarily in their own interests and those of manufacturers and their employees. Some citizens were advantaged but others were victimized. The created leadership runs in the same way as expressed by the theory of elitism. The leaders of this group always act focusing on the group interests and neglect the interest of others. In this way, democracy has become a demagogic plutocracy in the hands of created leaders. Demagogic plutocracy is a concept that refers to a system of government run by professional demagogues in their own interests and of those wealthy and other favoured groups (ibid.: 465).

Max Weber's theory of political leadership essentially relates itself with the concept of ethics and responsibility. He wants a kind of reconciliation of politics and ethics with the concept of responsibility. According to Weber, political leadership entails an active rather than a passive meditation of fate. The political leaders must neither live in passive acceptance or bitterness of disenchantment nor flee from reality, but instead measure up to the world as it really is in its daily routine (Nicholas 1997: 549).

Here Weber wants to throw light on the ethics of responsibility to be followed strictly by the political leaders. A political leader is responsible to developing the situation of his follower or country by exercising the power he holds. Weber again says:

> No ethics in the world can dodge the fact that in numerous instances the attainment of "good" ends is bound to the fact that one must be willing to pay the price of using morally dubious means or at least dangerous ones – and facing the possibility or even the probability of evil ramifications. From no ethics in the world can it be concluded when and to what extent the ethically good purpose "justifies" the ethically dangerous means and ramifications.
>
> – 1978: 121

Here the indication given by Weber in connection with ends and means must be justified ethically for the good a leader wants to reach. The ethics of responsibility is important as a political leader must have to comply with it. Basically, a leader aims to do good to others by following available means. So, it is a relative one, because it depends on the experience of a leader which he has gathered throughout his work by applying various available means to reach the goal. According to Weber:

> If one opts for the ethics of responsibility one also decides in favour of rationality as means-ends rationality.
>
> – Ibid.: 68

In his writing Weber demands that a political leader must constantly appraise and reappraise the means by which he wants to do justice to the responsibility conferred upon him by the power he enjoys. A political leader must have passionate involvement for his political adventure to eliminate the risk of striving for success and to clear the path of success. It is told that the success of political leadership depends on the responsible judgement of the political leader and in his or her ability not only to seek a practical reconciliation between politics and ethics but in taking an active stand for particular ultimate values. Their impossible demand entails a life of constant struggle.

The ethics of responsibility corresponds with the ethics of Kant. According to Kant:

> Acting such a way that you always treat humanity whether your own person or in the person of any other, never simply as a means, but always at the same time as an end. – 1991: 91

Here Kant clearly indicates that no person can be used as a means, but, should always consider a person as an end.

Now I want to consider the case of created leadership in democracy. As I have told earlier, created leadership is a different kind of leadership. It is not charismatic leadership as the leader does not have charismatic qualities. On the other hand, it is not transformational leadership or legal-rational leadership, at least in the first stage of its origin. This type of leadership is created or projected by others. In this case, the leadership has the following characteristics:

1. *Personal Interest:* Personal interest of the created leader is the goal of his or her predecessor. Personal interest means the interest to hand over the political power to a person of the same family so that this power can be used as an inherited quality. It is thought that the person who is selected as a leader is capable of exercising the powers conferred upon him by his predecessor.

2. *False Consciousness:* One kind of false consciousness is there in the concept of created leadership. A junior family member, who is selected as a leader, has the quality to apply political power in the political field like his or her predecessor. This type of thinking is nothing but a false consciousness. Without any experiment in the practical field the skill of the person is accepted here with a kind of expectation that this person will be able to lead the group of power holders successfully to reach the set goals. But in most of cases, the expectation transforms into disappointment.
3. *Lack of the Sense of Duty and Responsibility:* In created leadership, the leaders do not have the proper sense of their duty and responsibility. As they hold the power beyond their expectation and without any struggle they see only one side of the power and they ignore deliberately the other side, i.e. duty and responsibility.
4. *Fail to Create Personal Image:* In created leadership, the created leaders are always bound to stay under the umbrella of their predecessor. There is no scope to come out of the boundary set by the predecessor to create his or her fair and effective image to the followers. In this way they appear only as the shadow of the creator and in the long run they fail to achieve the goal of a successful leader.
5. *Scope to Misuse the Power:* The scope to misuse the legitimate power conferred upon the created leader is always there in the concept of created leadership, as they do not feel the need to exercise power for the benefit of others. There is a high chance to use the power for personal or sectional interest and in this way the created leaders may not follow the track set by their predecessor.
6. *Incorporation of Irrationality:* In created leadership there is a chance to neglect the ethics of responsibility while facing the reality and thereby there can be a shift from rationality of the ethics of responsibility.

General Observations

From the above discussion, it can be said that the concept of leadership is much more complex than it is thought. Leadership in political field, especially in the field of modern democracy, includes the idea of the ethics of responsibility. The success or failure depends solely on the capability of a leader to comply with the norms of the concept of ethics of responsibility at the time of exercising power. There is ethics of conviction as the opposite side of ethics of responsibility. The concept of ethics of conviction indicates the irrational conduct. In politics, it is desirable that leaders follow the ethics of responsibility for the good of others. If any leader drives his car of power to fulfil his own interests or to fulfil the interests of the followers surely he will be in the group of the ethics of conviction. It is true that the political leadership incorporates the sense of active role in the society. No political leader can remain passive in his field. Rather, he has to face the reality. According to Max Weber, a political leader must neither live in passive acceptance or bitterness of disenchantment nor flee from reality, but instead measure up to the world as it really is in its daily routine (Nicholas 1997: 549).

Here, Weber wants to put importance on the fact that a leader must have to face the ethical irrationality of the world and at the same time he has to take the responsibility for its comportment on political action. For, all political actions depend for their success on the ethical correspondence. In case of the concept of created leadership there is a high chance of a leader to act passively or to act differently when the world demands to act in a different way. It is also true that a created leader may not have the charismatic qualities to deal with the reality. So, either he has to depend on the office to use the power according to the advice of the bureaucrats or he will have to explain to the world in other ways according to his or her passion. So, ethics of responsibility will remain silent and he will have to choose the option of ethics of conviction instead of ethics of responsibility. The right path for a leader is to reconcile his/her passion and the ethics of responsibility. The big question arises in this critical juncture: Is it possible in the concept of created leadership? The future will answer this question.

References

Digeser, Petter, 1992, "The Fourth Face of Power", *Journal of Politics*, 54(4): 977-1007.

Kant, Immanuel, 1991, *The Moral Law: Grand Work of the Metaphysics of Moral*, London: Routledge.

———, 1996, *Ground Work of the Metaphysics of Morals*, tr. Mary Gregor and Jens Timmerman, Cambridge: Cambridge University Press (originally published in 1785).

Lukes, S., 1974, *Power: A Radical View*, London: Macmillan.

Morris, Peter, 2006, "Steven Lukes on the Concept of Power", Sage Journal, 1 May (journals.sagepub.com).

Nicholas, Gain, 1997, "Max Weber on the Ethical Irrationality of Political Leadership", *Sociology*, 31(3): 549-64.

Norman, Wintrop, 1992, "Elite Theory and Neo-Elite Theory Understanding of Democracy: An Analysis and Criticism", *Australian Journal of Political Science*, 27(3): 462-77.

Paige, Glenn D., 1977, *The Scientific Study of Political Leadership*, New York: The Free Press.

Rye, D., 2014, *Political Parties and the Concept of Power*, London: Palgrave Macmillan.

Thomson, Michel J., 2014, "False Consciousness Reconsidered: A Theory of Defective Social Cognition", *Critical Sociology*, 2 June, http: crs. sagepub.com

Weber, Max, 1978, *Economy and Society*, Berkeley, CA: University of California Press.

———, 2019, *Economy and Society: A New Translation by Keith Tribe*, London: Harvard University Press.

www.irmbrjournal.com (June 2013) *International Review of Management and Business Research*, 2(2).

Contributors

Jyotish Chandra Basak, Professor of Philosophy, teaches at the University of North Bengal. He keeps interests in Socio-political Philosophy, Ethics and Analytic Philosophy.

Kausik Bhattacharya, Associate Professor of Philosophy, teaches at the Department of Philosophy and Comparative Religion, Visva-Bharati, Santiniketan. His areas of interest are Contemporary Metaphysics, Continental Philosophy, etc.

Projit Kumar Palit, Professor of History, teaches at the Department of History, Assam University, Silcher. He has to his credit eight published books.

Samar Kumar Mondal, Professor of Philosophy, teaches at the Department of Philosophy, Jadavpur University and practises psychological counselling. He is also one of the Coordinators of the Centre for Counselling Services and Studies in Self-Development, Jadavpur University.

Gouri Sankar Bandyopadhyay, Associate Professor of History, serves as the Principal of Syamsundar College, Burdwan. He is also a senior faculty in History of Syamsundar College. He has authored sixteen books/monographs on different branches of social sciences: History, Religion and Culture.

Rajkumar Modak, Professor of Philosophy, teaches at the Department of Philosophy, Sidho-Kanho-Birsha University, Purulia. His areas of interest are Socio-political Philosophy, Ethics and Analytic Philosophy.

Tapan Kumar De, Professor of Philosophy, teaches at the Department of Philosophy, Vidyasagar University. His areas of interest are Socio-political Philosophy, Ethics and Continental Philosophy.

Index

a classless undifferentiated society, memory of 83
a democratic society, norms of 90
ability of decision-making procedure 117
absolute freedom 103
academic history of India 52
accountability 13
accounting
  laws 47
  management 46
  methodology 45
  principles, development of 45
  systems 52
accounting and financial
  management 45
  regulations 45
accusations of ineptitude or malfeasance 127
active participation of masses in political decision making 14
adequate standard of living 67
adharma 47
adhyakṣas 54
administrative
  law 59
  machinery 50
adulthood, definition of 28
advanced democracy 7, 39
  mark of 39
advanced technique of statecraft 50
Aeschylus 14
aggregative views of democracy 29
aggression, principles of 48
agreement of all and interest of all, distinction between 24
agricultural practice in India, genesis of 54
agronomy 55
ahiṁsā 110
  and love, the two soul forces of human being 109
Ajataśatru 78, 82, 86
all
  controllers, control of 41
  politics, fundamental problem of 41
Altekar, A.S. 46
Ambaṭṭhasutta 81
Ambedkar, B.R. 75-77, 79
Ambhi 48
Ambhīyas 48
an ideal state, structure of 105
Ananda 86

ancestral institutions 9
ancient
  Greek political and philosophical thought 4
  Indian
    civilization 43
    tax system 45
angry nationalism 35
animal welfare 52
anti-democratic authoritarian practices 9
ānvikṣikī 47
anyāya 47
aparāntanam 55
application of law 9
Arab Spring 32
archaic spirits of tribal democracies 84
Arendt, Hannah 121
aristocracy 3, 15
Aristotle 1, 7, 97-98
Arrow, Kenneth 30
art of
  diplomacy 7, 53
  politician 118
  statecraft 53
artha 47, 49, 51
artha-nīti 50
Arthaśāstra 7, 44-52, 55-58, 82
  defines one's life and the purpose of life 51
  main objective of 53
artificial distinctions between man and man 76
Aryan rule of life 49
Aśoka 46
aspects of crop cultivation 55
association group 85
associational autonomy 101
astrology-based-rain-forecast 55
Atharvaveda 43
atheist religion 90
Athenian democracy, father of 4
Audi, R. 66
authority of
  a chief minister of a state of India 129
  prime minister of India 129
autocratic
  rule 6
  state 5
autonomous principalities 82

Bachrach 123
bad governance 2
Bakunin, Mikhail Aleksandrovich 12
Balkundi, H.V. 54
Baratz 123
Barker, Ernest 71
Basham, A.L. 46
basic
  assumptions of a democratic society 91
  fabrics of democracy 6
  human rights 101, 104
belief in freedom and equality 96
Berlin Wall, collapse of 32
Bharadwāja 47-48
bhāṣya 48
Bhattacharjee, Biman 44, 46, 48-49, 51-52

Bhattacharya, K. 72
bhikkhu 88
Saṅgha 86
bhikkhus 80, 87, 89
bhikṣukī 57
bhoja 44
biggest socio-religious movement in Indian history 78
Board of Shipping 58
Bobbio, Norberto 100
Boesche, Roger 46, 48
bomb blast 42
Bose, A.N. 80
Bose, Netaji Subhas Chandra 17, 127
brāhmaṇas are inferior 81
Brahmāṇḍa Purāṇa 58
Brāhmanical
political thought 77
socio-religious rites and rituals 79
supremacy 90
Bṛhaspati 47-48, 50
broad aspect of nationalism 110
Bryce, Lord 64
Buddha, Gautama/Lord 8-9, 75-80, 82, 84-89, 91, 127
as a progressive socio-religious reformer 75
socialistic ideas of Gautama 8
Buddha's
concept of democracy 85
crusade against caste–class discrimination 78
ideal kingdom 83
Buddhism 8, 75-78, 80, 84, 90
as a democratic religion 77
important precepts of 81
is identical with European Protestantism or Lutheranism 77
meaning and intent of 91
wider popularity of 90
Buddhist
Bhikṣu Saṅghas 79
Canon Law 88
literature 75
materialism 90
Order 9, 80, 87
philosophy 90
political thought 77, 81
republicanism, ideal of 81
Saṅgha(s) 85, 87
tradition 83
Burke, Edmund 19-20, 28

Cāṇakya 44, 46, 51
Cāṇakya-Rājanītiśāstra 45
Cāṇakyasūtras 45
capitalism 13, 109
capitalist societies 66
cardinal principle in a democratic society 75
Carroll, Lewis 30
caste
discrimination 90
system 76
caste-based Brāhmanical socio-economic-political system 80
caste–class consciousness 9
casteism, principles denying 77
casteless monastic organization 75
Chaitanya, Sri 127

Chandrasekaran, P. 45
characteristics of
- democracy 5
- liberalism 16

charisma, routinization of 128
charismatic authority 126-27
- transformation of 128

charismatic leader 127-28
- power of a religious leader 126
- qualities 133

charismatic leadership 10, 115, 126, 130, 133
- concept of 126
- theological concept of 126

Chattopadhyay, D.P. 77-78, 82-85, 87-89, 91
choice, freedom of 102
Christ 85
Churchill, Winston 22
city-state 4
civil
- law 59
- rules 52
- societies 65

civil society 9, 102, 111-12
- concept of 111
- role of 110
- works as a support-giving mechanism 111

class exploitation 90
classical liberalism 65
classless
- democratic colonies 91
- society 72

Cleisthenes (or Clisthenes) 4
Clinton, Bill 127
clusters approach administration 53
codification of regulations and rules of accounting 45
Coḷa Empire 58
collapse
- of Berlin Wall 32
- process of 13

collective
- decision 30
- preferences 31
- righteousness 83
- welfare of common man 49

colonial ideology of nationalism 109
colonial-cum-materialistic approach 109
commercial transactions, law of 59
Commissioner of Port 58
common man, collective welfare of 49
communist ideology 34
communistic principles of private relations 88
compassion 90
concept of
- charismatic leadership 126
- civil society 111
- created leadership 134
- creative destruction 13
- false consciousness 124
- freedom 96
- objective interest 124
- responsibility 132
- right 66
- state 7

concept of democracy 6-7, 63, 89, 101
formation and 44
minimalist interpretation of 6
concept of ethics 115-17, 120, 123, 132
at the time of exercising power 10
concept of human
civilization 101
rights 68
concept of interest 123
is problematic 125
concept of leadership 117, 120, 129, 135
ethics of 119
concept of power 120-21
is not static 122
over 122-23
conception of
natural rights 28
society 85
conditions of good government 12
confederacy of the Vajjians 82
conflict of
interest 120, 124
subjective interest 125
Congress 89
consciousness, *dharma* of 76
constitutional
government 16
law 59
rights 112
contemporary
democratic process 100
political deliberations 12
contractualism 119
contradiction between education and learning 112
control of
all controllers 41
fraudulent accounting 45
conviction, ethics of 135
cooperative individuality 130
core
characteristic of democracy 14
of democracy 18
corruption 38-39
created leadership 115, 130-31, 134
concept of 134
in democracy 133
creating leader, process of 116
creation of laws 5
creative
brutality 117-18
destruction, concept of 13
imagination 117
leadership 130
crop cultivation, aspects of 55
Cullavagga 87
cultural and educational rights 105

dagana 57
Dahl, Robert A. 101, 123
Dalai Lama 84
daṇḍa 48
daṇḍa-nīti 50
daṇḍasalākā 87
Datta Majumdar, Shilpi 56-58
Dautrich, Kenneth 64
Davids, Rhys 75, 77-78

de Borda, Jean-Charles 30
de Condorcet, Nicolas 30
dead democracy 41
death of democracy 40
decayed democracy 39
decaying tribal republican communities 82
decision-making procedure, ability of 117
definition(s) of
  adulthood 28
  democracy 64, 97-98, 100
    given by Abraham Lincoln 64
delegate and a representative, distinction of 20
deliberative democracy 14
demagogic plutocracy 131
democracy 3-5, 11-12, 17-18, 22, 24, 37, 57, 63, 68, 71, 77, 91, 96
  aggregative views of 29
  and human rights, relation between 8, 68
  as political order 18
  basic fabrics of 6
  characteristics of 5
  concept of 6-7, 63, 89, 101
  core
    characteristic of 14
    of 18
  death of 40
  definition(s) of 64, 97-98, 100
  explanation of 72
  foreheads of 3
  forms of 64
  given by Abraham Lincoln, definition of 64
  ideal form of 112
  ideal(s) of 17, 63
  ideas of 82
  interpretations of 31
  necessary condition for 96
  notion of 13, 15
  oft-cited feature of 26
  paradox of 41
  parliamentary form of 6
  problem of 8, 69, 72
  problems in the establishment of 71
  requires three fundamental principles 4
  rule of 70
  schoolyard view of 29
  theoretical requirement of 25
  two chief features of 27
  variants of 5
  various shades of 6
  vital conditions of 100
  within Saṅgha 79
democracy as a
  form of governance 32
  political order 12
democracy is
  an ideal concept 100
  diffusion of power 99
  interrelated with human rights 68
  perversion of constitutional government 71
democracy is a
  form of institutionalization of continual conflicts 100
  political ideology 32
  rule by majority 64
  set of idea which is a principle about freedom 102
democracy's inner core 28
democratic
  administration, evolution of 14

atmosphere 40
attitude 16
culture 16
environment 77
ideals 15
ideas 75, 77
machinery is a tool for preventing rulers from acting arbitrarily 31
political order 28
procedure 12
regime 100
socialism 15
society, basic assumptions of 91
states 16
structures, six types of 12
system 115

democratic rights 37, 42
of
minority 42
tribes 42
violation of 7

democratic-representative form of government 107

dēmokratia 18
notion of 64

dēmos 15, 18, 20

Deogawank, Sangeeta 58

Derrida, Jacques 12, 33

deśavapanam 55

Deshkar, Sameer M. 53

despotism, possibility of 104

destruction of tribal republics 82

development of accounting principles 45

developmental policy 38

dhamma 83
doctrine of 90

Dhammarama, B. 80

Dhanānanda 44

dharma 8, 43, 46-47, 49, 76, 82, 91
of consciousness 76

dialectics, elements of 90

Dicey, A.V. 64

dictatorship 5

Digeser, Petter 124

Dīgha Nikāya 9, 79, 85

diplomacy 45
and kingship, principles of 50
art of 7, 53

direct democracy 13, 20, 69-70
and representative democracy, distinction between 19

Dīrghacyavana 48

disciplines, monastic code of 85

dispositional property 122

distinction between
agreement of all and interest of all 24
direct democracy and representative democracy 19
religion and politics 48
representative and delegate 19

distinction of a delegate and a representative 20

distribution for a socialist society, principle of 66

distributive justice 119

diverse social classes 19

divine power is called charisma 126

doctrine of *dhamma* 90

dogma of early Buddhism 90

driving force of the society 2
droṇamukha 53
dūtas 56
Dutt, Sukumar 85
dying democracy 38

early
    Buddhism, dogma of 90
    Buddhist philosophy 76
    Indian materialism 76, 85
economic
    equality 106
    growth and political stability 55
economics and government, science of 47
education 111-12
    and learning, contradiction between 112
effective participation 101
efficiency 37
    of the judiciary 38
efficient system of police and criminal administration 56
egalitarian
    and democratic ideology 9
    attitude of both Tathāgata Buddha and his unique monastic order 78
    collectivity and responsibility, ethos of 85
egoism 119
Ehrenberg, Victor 14
election process 103
electoral democracies 32
elements of dialectics 90
elephant taming, methods of 52
elitism 27
    in democracy, forms of 131
    theory of 131
elitists 31
emergence of the mass party 120
emissaries, functions of 48
end of
    history 6, 12
    ideological conflict 12
    ideologies 33
    justice should be the happiness of the common man 50
endism 35
endorsement through a referendum 25
Engels, Friedrich 84
enlightenment, notion of 102
entire Asia, history and culture of 8
environmental protection 66
    measures for 52
equal
    intrinsic value 107
    political rights 99
    status of power relation 122
equality 9, 13, 15-17, 27, 102
    before the law 106
    between the sexes 106
    ideal of 17
    in voting 101
    notion of 27
equality of
    all men, principles of 76
    income 107
    opportunity 106
    political influence 107
    respect 106-07
    people 96

eradication of racial inequality 67
espionage system 57
essence of a modern welfare state 8
essential feature of modern democracy 25
ethical
  irrationality 135
  norms of a leader 10
ethics 45
  and morality of urban living 52
  at the time of exercising power, concept of 10
  in politics, importance of 115
  concept of 115-17, 120, 123, 132
  rules of 120
  theories of 119
ethics of
  concept of leadership 119
  conviction 135
  Kant 133
ethics of responsibility 10, 115, 119, 132-35
  rationality of 134
  thread of 120
ethnicity 68
ethos of egalitarian collectivity and responsibility 85
evolution of
  democratic administration 14
  urban studies in ancient India 52
explanation of democracy 72
expression
  freedom of 101
  of human intelligence 48
extraordinary personal qualities 127
false consciousness 134
  concept of 124
  is the by-product of the concept of interest 125
family law 59
fare election 9
  process 97
father of Athenian democracy 4
feature of a pure and goodwill 119
first great political realist 48
fiscal policies 52
Fisher, Louis 117
five different schools of political thought 48
Flaig, Egon 87-88
Fleet, J.F. 46
forecasting on rainfall based on planetary movements 55
foreheads of democracy 3
foreign policy 48
formation and the concept of democracy 44
forms of
  democracy 64
  elitism in democracy 131
foundation of political and social thoughts of the Indian society 44
Fourth Estate 29
fraternity 15, 17
fraudulent accounting, control of 45
free and fare election(s) 101, 103-04
freedom 4, 9, 16-17, 44, 96
  concept of 96

movement 109
notion of 96
types of 103
freedom of
choice 102
expression 101
people 101
self-development 75
thought 102
French Revolution 28, 33, 63
Fukuyama, Francis 6, 12, 33-35
functions of emissaries 48
fundamental problem of
all politics 41
politics 72
fundamental right in India 28
fundamental rights 67, 76
of people 29
fundamentals of management 52

gahapati 81
gaṇas 9, 82
Gandhi, Mahatma (M.K.) 17, 109, 117, 127
Gandhian
concepts 117
nationalism 110
Ganges delta 57
gap between
ideal and actual democracy 98
individual and aggregate 31
what is ideal and what is real 106
gender discrimination 79
genesis of agricultural practice in India 54
Gettysburg Address 18
Ghotamukha 48
goals of society 48
God-gifted charisma 127
golden age of past 83
good governance 2-3
good government
and bad government, notion of 11
conditions of 12
gospel of tolerance 89
governance
mode of 15
of state 3
system of 2
government
and policy science, science of 45
of the people, by the people, and for the people 24, 64
monarchical form of 77
republican form of 77
grahapatikāvyāñjana 56
Gramsci, Antonio 111
Green, T.H. 65
group identity 16
growth of society 2
Gupta Empire 58
Gutmann, Amy 25-27

Habermas, Jurgen 111
Hamilton, Alexander 71
harmonious blending of might and wisdom 50
hedonism 119
Hegel, Georg Wilhelm Friedrich 65-66

hierarchy of spies 56

Hinduism 76

history

  and culture of entire Asia 8

  end of 6, 12

history of

  Homo sapiens 109

  Indian democracy 43

Hitler, Adolf 127

Holt, John Clifford 82, 85

Homo denisova 95

Homo erectus 95

Homo ergaster 95

Homo floresiensis 95

Homo neanderthalensis 95

Homo rudolfensis 95

Homo sapiens 95, 110

  history of 109

Homo soloensis 95

honesty 37-38, 48

horse training 52

horticulture 55

human

  civilization, concept of 101

  existence, three goals of 49

  intelligence, expression of 48

  liberty 75

human being as a rational animal 97

human beings

  intrinsic value of 111

  were the real capital of any nation 44

human rights 8-9, 47, 66-69

  concept of 68

  violation of 7

humanism, variants of 76

humanitarian intervention law 69

idea of

  law and power of justice 59

  nationalism 109

ideal

  and actual democracy, gap between 98

  democratic state 95

  form of democracy 112

  Saṅgha 89

ideal of

  Buddhist republicanism 81

  democracy 63

  equality 17

  liberty 65

  welfare of the people 70

ideals of

  democracy 17

  liberalism 16

ideas of democracy 82

identity

  politics 34

  yearning 35

ideological

  conflict, end of 12

  evolution 33

ideologies, end of 33

impartial judiciary 16, 49

imperial power 83

imperialistic expansion 85

importance of ethics in politics 115

important precepts of Buddhism 81

impure castes 81

incentive mechanisms 49
inclusive citizenship 101
income
  equality of 107
  redistribution 66
independence of judiciary 29
India
  academic history of 52
  naval supremacy of 58
Indian
  agricultural knowledge 54
  constitution 79, 104
  culture on other societies, widespread influence of 58
  democracy, history of 43
  history, product of 79
  political history 56
individual
  and aggregate, gap between 31
  inputs 31
individualism 65
Indus Valley Civilization 58
Industrial Revolution 63, 109
ineptitude or malfeasance, accusations of 127
infringement
  of people's democratic rights 40
  upon people's democratic right 37
inner soul force 110
inner-Saṅgha democracy 9, 87
institutional rights 67
integrity 37-38
intellectual freedom 102
interest
  concept of 123
  conflict of 120, 124
  is problematic, concept of 125
internal and foreign trade 52
international
  human rights law 69
  law 59
interpretations of democracy 31
intrinsic value of human beings 111
Islam 8
isothymia 34

Jaffrelot, Christophe 76
janapada kalyāṇī 79
Jātaka stories 58
Jayswal, K.P. 82, 86
joy of many people 78
judicial
  administration 48
  relief 38
  system, process of 103
judiciary 7
  independence of 29
  roles of 103
justice 15-16
  delayed is justice denied 108
  idea of law and power of 59
  notion of 17
  should be the happiness of the common man, end of 50

kāma 47, 49
Kangle, R.P. 47, 58
Kant, Immanuel 107, 111, 119, 133
  ethics of 133
Kantianism 119

Karl, Terry Lynn 101
Kātyāyana 48
Kaunapadanta 47
Kauṭilīya Arthaśāstra 56
Kauṭilya 7, 45-54, 56-59, 82
Kauṭilyan
  labour law 59
  secret service 57
  thought 59
Kauṭilya's state concept 44
Kennedy, John F. 127
khārvātika 53
khatriyas are superior 81
Khongchinda, Phramatachanya 80
Kierstead, James 88
kinetic power of a state 96
king and government, origin of 47
King Jr, Martin Luther 17, 127
kingship, tyranny is the perversion of 71
Kiñjalka 48
Kirthisinghe, Buddhadasa P. 89
koṣa 50
Kosambi, D.D. 45, 77
kratia 18
kratos 64, 80
Kropotkin, Peter 12
kulyavapaṇam 55

labouring population, wider masses of 118
Laslett, Peter 65
law
  and order, maintenance of 50
  application of 9
  misuse of 29
  process of 102
  rule of 3-4, 8, 29, 44
  system of 85
laws to govern commercial disputes 58
leader
  and followers, relation between 118
  ethical norms of 10
leaders, various types of 120
leadership
  and power, relation between 120
  concept of 117, 120, 129, 135
  in
    democracy 115
    political field 126
  process-based model of 130
  transformation of 130
  various dimensions of 117
legal
  equality 4, 44
  leadership 130
  rights 67
legal–rational leadership 10, 115, 133
legitimacy of ruling, principle of 21
legitimized rights 4
Leidecker, K.F. 91
Lenin, Vladimir 118
liberal
  political theory 66
  private property rights 49
  states 16
  value of liberty 29

liberalism 33, 65
- and democracy, tensions between 16
- characteristics of 16
- ideals of 16
- values of 16

liberal democracy 13-14, 33-34
- regressive movement of 34

libertarianism 65

liberties 4

liberty 13, 15, 17, 26-27, 32
- equality and fraternity, notion of 99
- ideal of 65
- liberal value of 29

life, Aryan rule of 49

Lincoln, Abraham 18, 64, 96, 127

lineage 77

living, adequate standard of 67

Locke, John 27, 65, 104

Lorenzetti, Ambrogio 11

love for truth 106

loving kindness 90

Lukes, S. 121, 124, 126

Macpherson, C.B. 16

Madison, James 121

Magadha 82

Magadhan Empire 78

Mahābhārata 63

Mahāparinibbānasuttanta 87

Mahāvagga 87

Mahāvastu Avadāna 83

Majjhima Nikāya 79

majority rule 6, 29

Majumdar, G.P. 55

Majumdar, R.C. 55, 82, 87

man
- and man, artificial distinctions between 76
- as part of social security, natural right of 28

management, fundamentals of 52

Mandela, Nelson 17

Mangrol Harbour 58

Manu 47-48, 50, 58

Manusmṛti 44

many people, joy of 78

maritime history 58

market correction 34

Marx, Karl 13, 33, 66

Marxian Theory, problem of 72

Marxist 41
- political thinker 111

Marxists 72-73

mass party, emergence of 120

masses in political decision making, active participation of 14

matsya yantra 58

Maurya 46, 58

Maurya, Candragupta 44-45, 50-51, 55

Mauryan period 55

Mazumder, R.C. 44

means–ends rationality 132

megalotthymia 34

Michel, Robert 120

Middle East 8

might and wisdom, harmonious blending of 50

military
  organization 48
  warfare 52
Mill, John Stuart 112
Miller, David 20
mind, talents of 119
mining 52
minority
  democratic rights of 42
  oppression of 42
Mishra, M. 47
model society 9, 91
modern democracy 16
  essential feature of 25
modern welfare state, essence of 8
mokṣa 47
monarchy 3, 15, 26
monastic order 82
Montesquieu, French Political Philosopher 26
moral
  and ethical standards 50
  code of a society 67
  law 67
  philosophy 32
  rights 67
morality ethics, principle of 118
Morris, Peter 122
Mosca, Gaetano 131

Nandas 44
Nandi, S.G. 46-47
Nārada 50
Narender Kumar 76
national unity 112
nationalism 102, 108
  broad aspect of 110
  colonial ideology of 109
  idea of 109
  narrow aspect of 109
natural
  law 66-67
  rights 28
nāvādhyakṣa 58
naval
  expeditions 58
  supremacy of India 58
  system 58
Nene, Y.L. 55
Nicholas, Gain 132, 135
nirvāṇa 76
Nisbet, H.B. 66
Nixon, President 39
no choice option 40
non-administrative people, quality of 37
non-discrimination, principle of 69
none found suitable option 40
non-political family members 116
non-proletarian working masses 118
non-violence 90
Norbu 82, 86
Norman, Wintrop 131
North Africa 8
nyāya 47

objective interest, concept of 124
Oldenberg, H. 78
oligarchy 4, 15, 71

is the perversion of aristocracy 71
Olivelle, Patrick 46
opportunity, equality of 106
opposition 102, 108
out-group enemies 118

pacittya offence 89
Padma, B. Sree 82, 85
Paige, Glenn D. 117-18
Pāli literature 75, 90-91
Palit, Projit Kumar 43, 46-47
Pāṇḍya Empire 58
Panebianco, Angelo 120-21
parachutism, theory of 116
Parāśara 47-48, 50
Pareto, Vilfredo 131
parliamentary democracy 12
    syndromes of 35
parliamentary form of democracy 6
parliamentary procedure 79
    rules of 79, 88
participatory democracy 13
party-less democracy 22
past, golden age of 83
Paul, Saint 126
pavaraṇa 85
peace 83
pedigree 77
Pelasgus, King 14
Peloponnesian War 21
Pennock, J. Roland 99
people
    equality of 96
    freedom of 101
    fundamental rights of 29
    quality of 37
people's democratic right(s)
    infringement of 40
    violation of 38
personal autonomy 14
perversion of aristocracy, oligarchy is 71
Piśūna 47
Piśūnaputra 48
Plato 7, 9, 17, 20-21, 23, 105-06
point-leadership and ethics 120
polarization 35
police and criminal administration, efficient system of 56
politeia 98
political
    and social thoughts of the Indian society, foundation of 44
    career 39
    consciousness 39
    democracy 77, 100
    equality 4, 106
    ideologies 11-12
    ideology, normative aspect of 32
    influence, equality of 107
    institutions 121
    judgement 19-20
    leader 116
    leadership 118, 135
        theory of 132
    organization 15
    philosophers 11

philosophy 11, 32, 80
Saṅgha 87
sciences 52
struggle, value of 116
terrorism 7, 38-41
thought
five different schools of 48
thought of Realism 48
politician, art of 118
politics 45, 52
fundamental problem of 72
main problem of 73
science of 49
Popper, Karl 5-6, 20-23, 25, 41, 72-73
popular
veto 31
will 13, 30
popularism 96
populist democracy 13-14
potestas in populo 121
power
coercion 122
concept of 120-21
holder 124
and source of the power, relationship between 122
relation, equal status of 122
source of 122
two-dimensional view of 123
power is
essential for perfect leadership 117
not static, concept of 122
power of
adaptability 95
appeasing the conflicts 100
execution 118
supreme authority of the party 131
tolerance 110
power over 122-23
concept of 122-23
powerful elite 35
powers
between different pillars of democracy, separation of 26
of king and feudatories 47
Pracetas Manu 48
Prajāpati, twin daughters of 43
prakr̥tis 47
prātimokṣa 85
president of India 129
primitive democracy 14
principle of
distribution for a socialist society 66
legitimacy of ruling 21
morality ethics 118
non-discrimination 69
principles denying casteism 77
principles of
aggression 48
diplomacy and kingship 50
equality of all men 76
taxation 48
private relations, communistic principles of 88
problem of
democracy 8, 69, 72
Marxian Theory 72
process of
collapse 13
creating leader 116
judicial system 103
law 102

separation of power 26
transformation 90
pro-democratic trend 33
professional demagogues 131
proportional representation 22
protection for
children 67
minority 67
women 67
Przeworski, Adam 100
public
administration 48
finance 48
pure and goodwill, feature of 119

qualitative brutality 118

racial
equality 106
inequality, eradication of 67
rainfall and soil classification 55
rājā 44
rāja-dharma 63
Rāmāyaṇa 58, 63
Rangarajan, L.N. 44, 47, 54
Raphael, D.D. 17, 24, 27
rasada 57
rational–legal authority 127, 129
Rawl, John 13, 119
Reagan, Ronald 127
realism, political thought of 48
refugee law 69
regional politics 131
regulations and rules of accounting, codification of 45
relation between
democracy and human rights 8, 68
leader and followers 118
leadership and power 120
relationship between power holder and source of the power 122
religion and
distributive justice 119
politics, distinction between 48
religion without God 90
religious
Saṅgha 87
tolerance 110
Renaissance 63
representation 13
representative 69
and delegate, distinction between 19
democracy 5, 25, 70
democratic state 5
government 16, 110
representative form of
democracy 99
democratic government 105
government 107
Republic 105
republican
city states 88
form of government 77
organization 82
respect, equality of 106-07
responsibility
concept of 132
ethics of 10, 115, 119, 132-35
revolution, theory of 72
Ṛgveda 58

right
  against exploitation 105
  concept of 66
right to
  constitutional remedies 105
  equality 104
  freedom of religion 105
  life and
    personal liberty 105
    physical integrity 69
  property 105
  six freedoms 104
  social security 67
rights
  of individuals 66
  types of 68
Riker, William 31
Roosevelt, Franklin D. 127
Roosevelt, Theodore 127
root of our social sufferings 72
Roper, Jan 99
Rousseau, Jean-Jacques 24, 30, 84, 112
royal consecration 47
rules on wars 47
Russell, Bertrand 12, 95
Rye, D. 120-21, 123

sabhā(s) 43-44
sacrificial rites 81
Śākya Muni 82
Śākyaputta 82
salākā 87
samāhartṛ 56
samitis 43-44
samrāṭ 44
saṁsthā 56
sāmya 85
Saṁyutta Nikāya 79
sañcāras 56
Saṅgam literature 58
Saṅgha 8, 75, 78-84, 86, 89-90
Saṅgha-induced democratic and socialistic ideas 91
saṅghaparināyaka 9
Saṅghas 9, 81-82, 85, 88, 90-91
saṅghatthera 9
saṅgrahaṇa 53
śāstra 46, 51
Sātavāhana Empire 58
sattrin 56
satyāgrahī 109
Schmitter, C. Philippe 101
Schumpeter, Joseph Alois 13
science of
  economics and government 47
  government and policy science 45
science of politics 49
science, rules of 45
Scott, Anthony 71
scripture of wealth 53
sea-borne traffic 58
secret service, two types of 56
self-annihilation 91
self-criticism 23
self-development, freedom of 75
self-imposed principles 96
self-satisfaction 65
Sen, Amartya 30
sense of identity 130

separation of power, process of 26
Sermon at Benares 90
seven qualities that lead to a republic's prosperity 86
Shamasastry, R. 46, 51, 54-55
Shapiro, Ian 101
short-time power 125
Sihag, B.S. 45
Sivaramakrishnan, A.S. 16
Smith, Anthony D. 108
social
  balance 31
  choice theory 30-31
  contract 84
  democracy 14
  democrats 14
  equality 106-07
  justice 15
  norms 4
  order 66
  philosophy 3
  process 120
  relations, skilful management of 117
  revolution 72
  security 42
  stratification and mobility systems 107
  structure 1, 45
  system 72
social and
  economic rights 67
  political revolutions 49
socialism 13, 15, 66
society
  conception of 85
  driving force of 2
  goals of 48
  growth of 2
socio-economic development of a state 47
socio-economical activities 47
Socrates 34
Son of the Śākyas 82
Spellmeyer, Kurt 89
spies, hierarchy of 56
spiritual progress 48
spiritualistic nationalism 109
spying designs 57
state
  concept of 7
  governance of 3
  unity and organization of 50
statecraft 13, 15, 45, 52
  advanced technique of 50
  art of 53
sthānīya 53
Strauss, Leo 15
strong infrastructure 49
subjective interest, conflict of 125
suffering, origin of 90
Sunitā 78
Supreme Court of India 7, 40
supreme legislative power 65
Sury, M.M. 46
Suu Kyi, Aung San 17

Tagore, Rabindranath 112
Talisse, R.B. 29-30
Talwar, P. 68-69
tapasāvyañjana 56
tathāgata 86

tax system 46-47
taxation 52
  principles of 48
  regulations 46
Teflon president 127
terrorism 42
Thakurdas, Frank 32
Thapar, Romila 45, 57
The Suppliants 14
Theragāthā 78
third-world countries 3
Thomson, Michel J. 125
thought, freedom of 102
three Vedas 49
tīkṣṇa 56
Tokarev, Sergei 76-77, 81, 90
tolerancc 15
  and education, values of 9
  gospel of 89
  pragmatism cooperation and compromise, values of 102
toleration 16-17
traditional
  authority 128
  leadership 10, 115, 131
transactional leadership 130
transformation, process of 90
transformational leader 129
transformational leadership 129, 133
  theory of 129
tribal democracies 83, 87
  archaic spirits of 84
tribal republics, destruction of 82
tribes, democratic rights of 42
triratna 8
trivarga 49
truth or righteousness, kingdom of 84
tyrannical rule 16
tyranny 5, 71

udasthita 56
ultimate, knowledge of 106
ultra-democratic constitution 87
United Nations Organization 67
  conventions 67
universal
  adult suffrage 28
  and eternal truth 128
universal Declaration of Human Rights 67
Upāli 78
upward control 4
urban
  living, ethics and morality of 52
  studies in ancient India, evolution of 52
US Declaration of Independence 28
Uśanas 47-48
utilitarian theory 124
utilitarianism 119
  theory of 119

vaidehakāvyāñjana 56
Vajjians 86
  confederacy of 82
value judgement 124
Vanhannen, Tatu 99
variety 15

varṇa(s) 49, 78, 83, 90
vārtā 47
Varuṇa 58
vassa 88
Vassakara 86
Vātavyādhi 47-48
Vedic
  age 43-44
  democracy 44
  philosophy 43
  tenets of harmony, equality, compassion and honesty 49
Vedic-Brāhmanical political thought 82
videśa-nīti 50
Vienna Declaration and Programme of Action 67
Vijayanagara Empire 58
vinaya 82, 85, 89
Vinaya Piṭaka 87
violence 40
violent revolution 13
virāṭ 44
Viśālākṣa 47-48
Viṣṇugupta 44, 51
Vivekananda, Swami 112, 127
Vṛjjis 82
vṛttiḥ 49

Warren, H.C. 85
Warwick Debates 108
Washington 127
Watergate scandal 39
Weale, Albert 99
wealth, scripture of 53
Weber, Max 10, 115, 126, 132, 135
Weber, May 128, 133
welfare and happiness of the majority of population 8
welfare of
  many people 78
  people, ideal of 70
Western liberal democracy, universalization of 33
what is ideal and what is real, gap between 106
Wood, Allen W. 66
working class 118
world conflict, threat of 69

Yalf, David A. 64
Yang, Larry 91